Fatal Attractions:

America's Youth and Their Affair with Alcohol

James E. Copple

LuLu Publishing, Inc.

ISBN 978-0-557-27448-2

Cover design by Ben Bartholomew,
RisingRain Studios.

ACKNOWLEDGMENTS

I have always enjoyed the art of writing but not always appreciated its discipline or craft. Professor Alice Spangenberg, retired Missionary and Professor of Freshman English at Eastern Nazarene College, grabbed me by the ear the second week of class and said, "Mr. Copple, a sentence is like a freight train, each word like a train car carries its own freight and has its own purpose. You must sweat every sentence and bleed every word." The ghost of Spangenberg has lived with me for nearly 30 years.

A book that seeks to blend research and translate research to practice requires conductors and engineers to build that train. There are so many who contributed to this book. My main compatriots in this effort have been Alan Rodda of Leadership Solutions who has edited and contributed to the logic model of the book, and Tracey D. Berger of Bingham Law was a major contributor. Tracey conducted field research on a number of College and University campuses. Her summaries of student interviews were riveting and revealing, and her capacity to press for the truth was compelling.

Chris Stoughton and Morgan Hester assisted with data collection and research analysis. Jim Gogek and Debbie Berger, both writers and editors of materials related to substance abuse, scrubbed the text looking for errors in grammar and research. Elizabeth Mattfeld and Kim Dalferes, colleagues and professionals in the field of substance abuse, read sections and raised important questions throughout the writing and editing process. Steve Edwards finally pushed me over the edge and said, "Get it done." Without his friendship and encouragement this project would still be on my laptop labeled DRAFT.

Finally, and for many of us men – it always comes down to this – there are three women whose contribution to my life have made the difference. My two daughters ,Jamie and Jessica, whose lives I have respected and whose experiences I have cherished, and Colleen - my partner, friend, coach, and navigator in so many different and wonderful ways, I offer thanks for your contribution.

At the end of the day, however, I stand alone on the shore bearing full responsibility for any errors or misdirection caused by the thinking or the writing found in this material.

DEDICATION:

I dedicate this book to Robert Reynolds, former Center Director at the Pacific Institute for Research and Evaluation. He was my mentor, my friend, and an advocate who pressed everyone to balance their passion with science. We fought, we laughed, and we disrupted a lot of conventional wisdom and practice about substance abuse. In this field, there has been no greater influence for those of us who believe advocacy should be both passionate and informed.

Table of Contents

Introduction

FATAL ATTRACTIONS: AMERICA'S YOUTH AND THEIR AFFAIR WITH ALCOHOL

Alcohol has been an important part of my life for as long as I can remember. I was nearly born in a bar, and on my birth certificate it identifies Grover's Tavern as my father's place of employment. It was also my mother's place of employment, too, and she was pregnant with me while working there. Early childhood memories for me aren't birthday parties, puppy dogs, and weekends at the beach, but watching my father walk through the door of our farm house in Kingsville, Missouri after he crashed his pick-up. Blood poured from gashes on his face as he staggered sideways. My horror at seeing my dad badly injured was mixed with my disgust and fear at seeing him drunk again. I knew the signs.

When I was nine, our baby sitter asked me to bicycle down to the store to buy her some cigarettes. I remember approaching an intersection, and the next thing I knew, I was lying on my back in the middle of the road. My bicycle was twisted and smashed. Nearby was the car that hit me with a woman slumped over the wheel of the car. Passers-by carried me into the passenger side of the car to keep me from freezing in the cold until help arrived. As consciousness dawned on me, I saw next to me on the car seat three empty bottles of liquor identical to the ones in my dad's liquor cabinet. The driver was passed out; she reeked of booze. An ambulance took me to the hospital, where I stayed for three days with a concussion and broken ribs. The drunk driver was ticketed for speeding and released. My father sued for a new bicycle and won.

Throughout my adolescence, I watched my parents struggle as the household finances never matched the bills and listened as their marriage deteriorated in loud quarrels and angry fights. I knew from a very early age that the cause was alcohol; it was central to everything in their lives – and consequently in my life. At family gatherings, parties with neighbors and friends, or evenings at home before the television, alcohol was there. At each occasion, as drinking progressed, children were ignored. Watching our parents' actions, and then left on our own, we naturally mimicked them, and began sampling the drinks left sitting on the tables.

At this point in the story, you probably think I'm going to start telling my own story of a tragic spiral into alcoholism with a hope-filled ending of redemption through a sober life. But it didn't turn out that way. Whether because of a quirk of genetics, the blessings of transformative spirituality, or pure luck, I did not become an alcoholic. In fact, I've always been a normal drinker, meaning I have a glass of bourbon or a beer every now and then. So I can't regale you with drunkalogues, and I won't hector you about temperance and abstinence, nor will I try to provide moralistic witness so that you can avoid my childhood fate. Instead, this book is about how the collective "we" can make some basic and often simple changes that will create a community-wide, and eventually a society-wide, protective system for our young people. They must be protected from the dangers of alcohol.

As I grew into my teens, my father's behavior increasingly embarrassed me, so I withdrew from him, and rarely engaged him at all. When I did, it was usually in anger. My father was an iconic figure and a man I greatly admired. He taught us lessons about living and working hard, but his use of alcohol was forever a disruption in our communication, and whenever he was drinking, there was always a tension in the room that made all things uncomfortable. Eventually, I would watch him die at the age of 68 with liver cancer, a direct result of his alcohol consumption. He was one of the statistics for the year 1992, one of 110,000 people who died that year as a result of alcohol consumption. But you don't have to be a late-stage alcoholic to die from alcohol. Among those 110,000 deaths were sons and daughters, more than a thousand college kids, prom kings or queens, high school football players, marching band members, skate-boarders, Sunday schoolers, infants, and more. Dying from alcohol doesn't usually mean dying from the deleterious effects of too much alcohol on the body. There are thousands of ways for the effects of alcohol to kill, maim, and injure, and young people are among the most vulnerable victims.

Consider:

- Alcohol is a leading cause of death among youth. It contributes substantially to adolescent motor vehicle crashes, other traumatic injuries, suicide, date rape, and family and school problems.[1]

- Underage drinking is a factor in nearly half of all teen automobile crashes, the leading cause of death among teenagers.[2]
- Alcohol is by far the most used and abused drug among America's teenagers. According to a national survey, more than one quarter (26 percent) of all high school students reported hazardous drinking (5 or more drinks in one setting) during the 30 days preceding the survey.[3]
- Approximately 10 million American youth under the age of 21 drink alcohol. More than half of them drink to excess, consuming five or more drinks in a row, one or more times in a two-week period.[4]
- Every day in the United States, 7,000 kids under age 16 have their first full drink of alcohol.[5]
- Children who drink alcohol by 7th grade are more likely to report academic problems, substance use, and delinquent behavior in both middle school and high school.

- Early alcohol use is associated with employment problems, other substance abuse, and criminal and other violent behavior.[6]
- Young people who begin drinking before age 14 are five times more likely to develop alcoholism than those who begin drinking at 21.[7]

The statistics can be mind numbing and cause us to glaze over the realities of the individual stories behind the data. People read these statistics and grasp their meaning but still pay them no heed. That's because youth drinking is so ingrained in our culture that it is tacitly accepted, even by those who know it's a severe problem. Even after everything we know, youth drinking is still considered a rite of passage. And we all know why. Alcohol is extensively glamorized through all forms of media to those who are the biggest media consumers – young people. But the reality of youth drinking – the horror of a midnight call to the emergency room or of lives crushed by long-term abuse – is not portrayed in alcohol marketing campaigns.

Jeff Levy, a retired Air Force fighter pilot, experienced this terrible reality. No battlefield training could have prepared him for the emotional trauma he suffered on the day his son Jonathan, a 20-year-old sophomore at Virginia's Radford University, was killed in a drunken driving crash. Jonathan was a passenger in a car driven by a drunken 19-year-old Virginia Tech student who Jon hardly knew. The driver, who was supposed to be the sober designated driver that night, was also killed. A third student in the car, who was also drunk, was critically injured and remained in hospitals and a rehabilitation facility for more than two years with brain damage, loss of an eye and part of a foot, multiple broken bones, and internal injuries.

According to witnesses, the car was being driven recklessly at 80 to 95 miles per hour on a secondary road connecting Radford and Virginia Tech. The driver lost control of the car and slammed head-on into another car, killing its driver, a professor at Radford who recently had completed her doctorate degree at Virginia Tech. The professor, who left behind a disabled husband and five adult children, was not a drinker.

But that was only the beginning of the devastation caused by this fatal crash. A few weeks later, Jon's best friend, suffering deep depression over the death, committed suicide. Jonathan's girlfriend, who had refused to get into the car with Jonathan because the driver was drunk, subsequently suffered a serious breakdown, dropped out of school, and was under medical treatment for years thereafter. Two other young people who were close friends of Jonathan suffered from serious depression. The effect of these three intoxicated young men getting into a car left an incalculable trail of emotional distress and loss.

In the year following his son's death, Jeff Levy visited universities to observe student drinking at parties, fraternity events, football games, and college town bars. He found that binge drinking was everywhere; there were no limits to risk taking. He saw the alcohol industry promotion of over-consumption among college-age drinkers by sponsoring Age 21 parties while flooding bars and taverns in college towns with drink promotions that encourage binge drinking. Jeff saw how students in most college towns are inundated with alcohol advertising and promotion which in turn creates immense peer pressure and second-hand affects – such as being the victim of alcohol-related assaults and sexual assaults. And, he saw how any efforts to curb these problem-causing activities were met with strong resistance from chambers of commerce, bar and liquor store owners, beer wholesalers, the alcohol industry, and local policy makers.

Jeff saw that the solution to the problem is within our grasp; in fact, we already know how to do it. But, it certainly is not easy. He joins me and many others who believe that we need to build a protective system for young people to guard against alcohol problems, and we need to change the culture that says youth drinking is okay.[8]

We've built protective systems for other risks, and they've worked out well, (i.e. problem driving). When traffic deaths and injuries became a glaring problem decades ago, we didn't throw up our hands and say that nothing could be done about it, that people were going to drive dangerously no matter what, and that young people driving recklessly is a rite of passage. Nor did we look for one single solution and then turn defeatist when it didn't immediately work. Yet, those are popular reactions to youth drinking today.

Instead, when faced with growing deaths and injuries from an increasing number of vehicles on our roads and the concurrent increase in dangerous driving, we built a protective system that works, considering the huge numbers of drivers on the road. Think of all the protections we have today for drivers, passengers, and pedestrians: auto safety design, traffic laws and enforcement, street and highway design, traffic signals and signs, seat belts and air bags, driver's licensing and testing, graduated licenses for youths, strict drunk driving laws, etc. And, a culture of safety has been built around motor vehicle use by government, schools, law enforcement, car makers, and others. And it's worked. The per capita number of traffic fatalities has steadily declined[9] as have traffic injuries[10]. About 1 million fewer people were injured in traffic crashes in 2008 than in 1997. Most importantly, this protective system is always improving. Nobody would dream of saying, "Streets and highways are safe enough with only 37,000 killed and 2.3 million injured each year. Our job is done."

Why can't we also build a protective system around problem drinking and youth drinking? Mobilize systems to prevent teenage drinking so that we can reduce the 110,000 dead and millions of injuries each year from alcohol. Why can't we change that insane statistic that nearly half of all patients in hospitals are there because of trauma and disease caused by alcohol abuse?[11] And, most importantly, why can't we lessen the chances that loving fathers like Jeff Levy must bury their sons?

To succeed, we must confront two challenges. One challenge is found in the alcohol industry. Those who produce, distribute, and sell alcohol are often the main roadblocks to reducing problem drinking and protecting our youth. The purveyors of these products spend a lot of money telling people to drink responsibly and even set up foundations to prevent underage drinking. Then, they turn right around and simultaneously promote products that taste like soda pop using cartoonish characters, music popular with teens, and other images meant to entice youth. They encourage binge drinking in college town bars while mouthing the words "drink responsibly". They obfuscate real knowledge about problem drinking by creating their own data on alcohol. They have enormous influence in Congress, state Legislatures, county seats, and city halls.

The second challenge is us! Parents and families need to quit candy-coating the problems of alcohol use by young people -- deaths, injuries, wasted lives, and the collateral damage to families and communities. Rather than acceptance of the status quo, we need to get mad as hell. Undue youth attraction to alcohol can be dulled, and the fatal or injurious consequences of their relationship to alcohol are both preventable and treatable.

This book examines the problems associated with alcohol consumption among youth and the impact of the alcohol industry and popular culture on youth drinking. Throughout, it suggests specific strategies for parents, families, and communities to enable sustainable change and prevent this problem from becoming a more widespread and possibly even a personal tragedy. Please take this information seriously. The most tragic words in the world are people, especially family, saying: "If only I had done something to stop this..."

The fact is that there are things you can do and actions you can take that will eliminate alcohol consumption among our youth. Start today! The fatal attractions of youth to alcohol are preventable – if only we will engage the battle. You will find many ways to make a difference.

Questions To Ponder As We Begin This Journey

1. What is your earliest memory of alcohol consumption?
2. How has alcohol directly impacted your life? Think of relatives, friends, or colleagues whose alcohol consumption impacted your life.
3. What are the messages communicated to you by parents regarding alcohol use or consumption?
4. Can you identify a marketing or advertising vehicle by the alcohol industry that you feel is aimed at youth?
5. What is the message you want to communicate to young people regarding alcohol and alcohol consumption?

1 – THE FATAL ATTRACTION

The defense attorney stood before a judge in Green Bay, Wisconsin and tried to justify the behavior of his client, a 19-year-old who had shot to death another youth while in a drunken rage. The attorney explained that his client "had been drinking. He shouldn't have been – after all, he was underage. But, you know kids. They all try it." The attorney went on to explain that, when his client drank, he lost control of his temper and his actions. But he drank anyway. If he hadn't been drinking, this tragedy wouldn't have happened, he said.

The murder was horrific enough. But when placed within the popularly accepted inevitability of youth drinking, it shows how flawed our assumptions are and to what sick lengths we, as a society, will go to advance the absurd claim that kids are always going to drink no matter what. This is a myth of unknown origin perpetuated by people who either want to believe it or haven't taken the time to consider what they're saying. People say we'll never stop underage drinking, but that's a red herring – a diverting argument meant only to derail discussion of what's really important. Prevention is not about completely stopping any risk behavior, whether it's dangerous driving, tobacco use, unsafe sex, or even jaywalking. We'd never say, for example, you can't stop dangerous driving, so why bother trying? The fact is that we can significantly reduce underage drinking, and thereby save lives, reduce injuries, cut public costs, and alleviate the heart-ache of spouses, children, or friends killed or injured by drunken youths. We already know how to do it, but we must start taking it more seriously and truly believe that we can do it.

To begin, we need to agree on why we must prevent youth drinking. Let's start by considering the victims, who are not just the people killed as a result of underage drinking, but all of us. The "every kid does it" defense offers little consolation to the psychologically injured family of the above murder victim or the thousands of victims who are killed or injured by youth drinkers who get behind the wheel, assault somebody, or engage in risky sex or acquaintance rape. And it is not only the victim, if he or she lives, but also the victim's family who must recover. The lasting consequences in the life of the youth drinker and his or her family can be equally terrible. In the Wisconsin drunken murder, the victim had two siblings and the shooter had four. All of them innocently lost a brother – one to death and the other to prison. The shooter was convicted of murder and will spend the rest of his life in prison at an estimated cost of $30,000 a year for his incarceration. If the shooter lives to be 65, it will cost the citizens of Wisconsin nearly $1.4 million. And, this is one event in one community in one state. Dangerous alcohol-fueled events by underage drinkers occur many times each day in our nation. According to the National Institute on Alcohol Abuse and Alcoholism, about 5,000 people under the age of 21 die each year from drinking, mostly from car crashes and homicides. That's nearly 14 a day. And that doesn't count the hundreds of thousands of injuries, assaults, sexual assaults, property crime, or even the Ds and Fs on report cards that are a result of underage drinking.

The costs of underage drinking are substantial. The National Academy of Sciences (NAS), Institute of Medicine released a landmark report to Congress in September 2003, "Reducing Underage Drinking: A Collective Responsibility", which found that underage alcohol use costs the nation an estimated $53 billion annually.[12] By 2005, that cost had increased to $60.3 billion, annually. [13]

The Cost of Underage Drinking [14]

Youth Violence:	$31,100,000
Youth Traffic Crashes:	$14,900,000
High Risk Sex, Ages 14-20	$5,600,000
Youth Property Crime:	$3,100,000
Youth Injury:	$1,900,000
Poisonings and Psychosis:	$500,000
Fetal Alcohol Syndrome Among Mothers 15-20	$1,100,000
Youth Alcohol Treatment:	$2,200,000
TOTAL:	**$60,400,000**

Another report estimates that societal costs associated with underage drinking are nearly $62 billion.[15] Meanwhile, there are other shocking statistics. Teenage girls who binge drink are up to 63 percent more likely to become teen mothers.[16] More than 70,000 college students are victims of alcohol-related sexual assault or date rape each year.[17] Half a million college students are injured each year while under the influence of alcohol.[18]

The data on the human and financial costs of underage drinking goes on and on. All of the research documenting the evidence on its terrible consequences could not possibly be quoted in this chapter or book. One would think that 5,000 deaths of young people each year – over 2,000 more than died in the 9/11 attacks – would energize everybody to demand effective action. The top federal government authorities should be enacting aggressive efforts through executive agencies, and Congress should be passing tough new laws. While 5,000 people die as a result of underage drinking, a total of 100,000 Americans die each year from alcohol.[19] That's nearly three 9/11s every month! Where's the outrage?

The outrage is mute or nonexistent. Why? In part, it is because of the enormous amount of advertising, promotion, and sponsorship by the multi-pronged alcohol industry that created and perpetuates the fatal attraction by convincing people that alcohol is a desirable, necessary, and vital part of the good life for adults and youth. The truth is that alcohol is a mind and body altering drug/beverage.

While the alcohol industry boasts of its commitment to responsible drinking and reducing underage consumption, youth drinking provides significant revenues for the alcohol industry. According to studies conducted at the Pacific Institute for Research and Evaluation, underage drinking accounted for 16 percent of alcohol sales in 2001.[20] The Center on Addiction and Substance Abuse at Columbia University estimates that the percentage of alcohol sales to underage drinkers accounts for 37.5 percent.[21] Halting underage drinking in America would eliminate at least $48 billion in annual profits for the alcohol industry.

Meanwhile, the alcohol industry contributes less than $10 million to social responsibility messaging (Designated Driver, and Friends Don't Let Friends Drive Drunk Campaigns) although they also contribute that often-lampooned throw-away line "please drink responsibly" to their advertisements. The efficacy of these industry campaigns has been questioned by many research reports. Forgive me if I'm skeptical about the industry's social responsibility efforts. It appears, from the massive youth-oriented marketing and billions of dollars in sales incentives, that reducing underage drinking is not something the alcohol industry really wants to do.

A closer look at some of the specific "grief-to-benefit ratios" found in alcohol profits and alcohol costs supports this skepticism:

Anheuser-Busch InBev [22]

Total Revenue (2008): €16.1 Billion (approximately $23.57 Billion[23])

Normalized Profit (2008): €4.02 Billion (approximately $5.89 Billion)

Estimated Sales to Underage Youth: €1.77 Billion[24] (approximately $2.59 Billion)

Estimated Profit from Sales to Underage Youth: €442.2 Million (approximately $647.44 Million)

U.S. Advertising Spending (2003): $266.7 Million[25]

Molson Coors Brewing Company[26]

Net Sales (2008): $4.77 Billion

Income from Continuing Operations (2008): $400.1 Million

Estimated Sales to Underage Youth: $524.7 Million

Estimated Profit from Sales to Underage Youth: $44.01 Million

Diageo PLC[27]

Total Sales (2008): £8.09 Billion (approximately $15.89 Billion[28])

Operating Profit (2008): £2.3 Billion (approximately $4.52 Billion)

Estimated Sales to Underage Youth: £889.9 Million (approximately $1.75 Billion)

Estimated Profit from Sales to Underage Youth: £253 Million (approximately $497.05 Million)

SABMiller PLC[29]

Total Revenue (2009): $18.7 Billion

Operating Profit (2009): $3.15 Billion

Estimated Sales to Underage youth: $2.06 Billion

Estimated Profit from Sales to Underage Youth: $34.65 Million

U.S. Advertising Spending (2009): $255.7 Million

To further demonstrate the duplicity of this behavior, the Century Council, the prevention organization for the spirits lobby, and the Beer Institute claim that their social responsibility campaigns are working. Not so fast.

The kind of prevention programs sponsored by the alcohol industry, usually involving exhorting people not to drive drunk or to only drink responsibly, have not led to good outcomes according to the scientific evaluators. On the other hand, prevention strategies involving policy change and enforcement, particularly those involving price and access, have shown scientific evidence of success, although the industry abhors them because they cut into profits. Further, the data is clear that enforcement of underage drinking laws yields greater return on our prevention and intervention efforts. Senator Robert Byrd of West Virginia has long championed the congressionally-funded initiative called Enforcing Underage Drinking Laws (EUDL) providing states with approximately $400,000 a year to help develop laws and enforce the laws. That program has contributed to saving thousands of lives in its ten year history. Enforcement of policy in local communities and in the states has greater impact than all of the combined social marketing efforts of the alcohol industry.

Unfortunately, public health and community groups don't have a great track record, either. The public health field is adrift in its many instances of organizational impotence. Many agencies that undertake prevention advocacy are still embracing strategies that address only individual behaviors that rely on education alone to change population-wide behaviors. Despite the fact that well-established research shows that these largely fail, many communities still rely on the equivalent of tying ribbons around trees to address youth alcohol and drug use.

Making matters worse, we have otherwise intelligent people, including some college presidents, claiming that lowering the drinking age would actually reduce underage drinking problems. There is no scientific evidence to back up these claims, and there's plenty of evidence to refute them. The minimum legal drinking age of 21 has saved a lot of lives. Between 1982 and 2004, at a time when states were raising drinking ages from 18 to 21, the number of fatal crashes involving drinking drivers under age 21 fell nearly twice as fast as for drinking drivers over 21.[30]

One is tempted to think that college and university presidents are tired of being held accountable for underage and binge drinking on their campuses and believe that if they just make it legal, they can get out of the spotlight. Whatever they intend, research clearly shows that much worse will happen: the morbid statistics will be worse and more students will suffer. In New Zealand, when the drinking age was lowered from 20 to 18, car crashes involving 15-19 year olds significantly increased as did emergency room admittance and disorderly conduct among this age group.[31] The college and university presidents, deans, and regents who support lowering the drinking age are buying themselves trouble while confusing the public and parents as to the truth about underage drinking. According to the Harvard School of Public Health's 2009 College Alcohol Study results, (CAS) director Henry Wechsler says, "Lowering the drinking age would be like using gasoline to put the fire out." "College presidents do need more help," Wechsler says. "But instead of giving up, they should join forces with the community. They've got to strengthen existing policies and restrict easy access to alcohol."

Though there is an excellent library of research on the problems of and solutions for youth drinking and alcohol abuse, often science does not help by providing a clear picture of the true public health environment surrounding alcohol use. Instead, the net effect is to muddy the water. For example, anyone who reads the news is probably familiar with the conflicting reports routinely published in newspapers and on news websites about whether or not alcohol is good for your health. There's probably enough evidence to stipulate that a small glass of wine may have cardiovascular or other health benefits for some people. Yet, what is disarming about these studies is that they tend to eliminate or obscure the health statistics and global harm of over-consumption of alcohol.

The health benefits of an occasional glass of wine have no bearing on the two million deaths worldwide from alcohol or the multiple millions of crimes and injuries related to alcohol. Nor do the health benefits speak to the fact that in this country 15 percent of all individuals who consume alcohol will develop alcohol dependence. A small glass of wine or two may be fine - if you're not an alcoholic or underage. And what about two or three glasses of wine and then driving your car, using power tools, or going to work as a subway conductor? What are the associated health and safety risks? The research doesn't say, because the context of real life isn't one of the variables in their "scientific" studies.

Are we prepared to accept the real human and economic costs associated with alcohol use and weigh them against the benefits of occasional consumption of alcohol? No, or at least, not yet. The fatal attraction with alcohol is marked by our inability or refusal to acknowledge and address the real-life health and safety risks of alcohol.

Without strong intervention and with major industries and special interests promoting underage drinking in almost every quarter of our society, the problem of youth drinking will never significantly improve and may very well get worse. The promotional message is that widespread and significant consumption of alcohol has always been part of the cultural and social norm of America, when the truth is that most American adults abstain from drinking or drink very little.[32] The industry wants us to believe that alcohol consumption is just normal or expected behavior among youth. They want us to wink and nod about youth drinking and accept it as a rite of passage. Parents are counseled to make "no big-deal" out of kids' experimentation with alcohol.

In her own words, Alison Servino of Erie, Pennsylvania, described how she almost died from alcohol poisoning when drinking at a post-prom party: "I'm seventeen years old, and at the age of fourteen I almost died of alcohol poisoning. It was my freshman year in high school, and I was invited to the prom by a senior. I went to the prom and afterwards, I went to an after-prom party, which was only a neighbor's house away. At the party, I began drinking. I had one beer, and two beers, and then a few wine coolers.

Then a few wine coolers led to an entire bottle of vodka. I downed the bottle of vodka and suddenly went into a coma. My friends decided that the only thing that they knew that they could do was to drag me upstairs and try to give me a cold shower to see if I would come to. Instead of coming to, it made me worse. They threw me in the back of a pickup truck and they left me there. No one did anything. No one called my parents. I began to go into convulsions from the amount of alcohol I consumed. They called the rescue squad, and they came and got me. I almost died in the ambulance on the way to the hospital."

Alison made choices, her friends made choices, the neighbors in the community made choices, and because this was associated with a prom event, the school and parents made choices. Where were the adults? Any time that a 14-year-old – or any underage youth -- consumes alcohol, an adult is involved, either in selling or providing the alcohol. Somewhere along the line, Alison was the victim of a complicit adult.

Nora Drexler, one of our country's leading activists and coalition leaders, was a victim as well, though a different kind of victim: "Having just left a peaceful church service at 6 p.m. on a tranquil, cricket-laced summer evening, my husband and I headed to what should have been a festive evening at my 25th high school class reunion. However, the screeching sounds of sirens and emergency vehicles shattered the reality of a reunion with classmates. Our vehicle was broadsided by a half-ton pick-up truck that sped through a stop sign. At the helm of the truck was an underage drinker. Our vehicle was demolished. I still shudder when I remember the elegant, flowing, evening gown, being cut off of me in the emergency room. More than 300 pieces of glass were imbedded in my skin and shimmering over my body... glistening in the hospital lights. I had several surgeries as a result of the injuries, over a period of two years, including the implantation of a cardiac pacemaker. I now have no natural heart rhythm."

The problem we face is that neither the statistics nor these real-life tragedies have much impact against the avalanche of advertising, marketing, and promotion that dominates the social landscape of alcohol and creates the fatal attraction of alcohol to youth. I saw that attraction up close one night when I had dinner with a group of young people at a family and community social event. This event included many young people who were either under the age of 21 or were in their early 20s. After dinner, I sat with the young men in the group. Two of these young men were in law school, one was in medical school, another was a realtor, another studying to be a chef, and the last was a sailor. They were all experienced drinkers, and I knew they had been drinking since high school. I asked them to tell me when they took their first drink. All six had started drinking before the age of 14.

I enjoyed their company but was saddened as I watched them binge drink the whole evening. Of the group that evening (male and female), all of them drank. They have developed drinking patterns and habits. They know what they like and what they don't like. They name the weaknesses and strengths of various brands of beer, wine, and bourbon. As the evening wore on, I watched their inhibitions disappear, their laughter grow louder, and their conversations become more absurd. I was embarrassed by their behavior and choices. I began wondering which of them would become alcoholics, which would continue heavy drinking until it caused real problems in their lives or families, and which would truly moderate before it was too late.

As the evening wore on, I listened to their stories of near escapes and of embarrassing moments related to their alcohol consumption. There was shame, pride, and the typical youth bravado associated with escaping death. Out with their friends and with the alcohol flowing, they lost control and miraculously escaped danger then bragged about the horrible hang-over the next morning. They talked about almost falling off a cliff, falling down while darting across a busy street, and being in a car driven by an out-of-control driver. I could not help but speculate on other behaviors they were not discussing. How many of them had unprotected sex while under the influence of alcohol, how many relationships were destroyed by the chronic use and presence of alcohol at their events, or how many relatives were embarrassed by their alcohol consumption? Those were not discussed, because even in that setting and under the influence of alcohol, they showed some discretion.

Social scientists accurately calculate the deaths, injuries, and health consequences of alcohol-related risky behaviors. But, what if they and we were to calculate the millions of near misses associated with the alcohol consumption of youth?

When it comes to alcohol, health and safety is all about the percentage of risk involved. When you add alcohol to most situations, the probability of injury, disease, or death increases dramatically. This is the straight forward formula for potential disaster. More alcohol plus youthful bravado and every day hazards such as driving inevitably raise the percentage of risks of a significant catastrophe happening that will affect many throughout their lives.

As I looked at those 14 young people that evening, I became nearly certain that tragedy would visit some of them because of alcohol. I feared there was a funeral waiting to happen among them or a funeral in the life of a family that was a part of the consequences of their alcohol consumption.

I asked myself, "Why is alcohol so important in so many people's lives, especially young people?" Is the effect of alcohol, the romance of alcohol, and the lore and lure of alcohol really worth more than an occasional mug of beer or glass of wine? Is consuming a great quantity (or any quantity if you are under the age of 21) of a liquid really worth risking a life? How can it possibly be measured against the loss of a friend, a child, or brother or sister, or against killing or maiming someone while drunk?

Despite the fact that our society is inundated with messages promoting alcohol use among youth, I believe that there is still hope. Those of us engaged in this fight against an industry that is willing to spend hundreds of millions to convince more people to drink and to consume greater quantities, we know for certain that we can and will save lives. We really have nothing to lose and everything to gain by our efforts to combat underage drinking. We are making progress in changing the behavior and actions of an alcohol industry often more concerned with market share than market survival. Recently, Beam Wine and Spirits modified their advertising exposure rates to prevent underage viewers on television from seeing any of their commercials or promotions. Beam worked in collaboration with the National Association of Attorneys General to keep alcohol promotions away from youthful viewers. They were criticized by the Distilled Spirits Council (their trade association) for caving into the pressure applied by prevention organizations. Beam has since become an important partner and funder of many new prevention strategies designed to keep alcohol away from young people. They have a long way to go before convincing the prevention community that they are serious - but it is a start. I am certain that they and others will continue to move in this direction as long as we have the Nora Drexlers and Jeff Levys working in this field.

Note the spirit and courage of Nora Drexler:

"Since implantation of my pacemaker, I now greet each new day as a special, "gift-wrapped package." Each morning when I awake, I believe that

I have been issued a special Visitor's Pass for at least one more day... one more day of hugs and smiles and wonderful youth and adult coalition members and lawmakers fighting hard to reduce and prevent underage drinking. I have led coalitions for ten years, initiating Project: Sticker Shock, an alcohol warning labeling campaign; Project: unBEARable, a vehicle-labeling campaign with alcohol enforcement messages; and I have rolled beer kegs two miles and up capitol steps to get alcohol compliance checks passed in a state legislature. The smiles of those fighting underage drinking are etched on my heart forever. The fight is never-ending, but it is worth every minute."

Nora is a mom, a teacher, a church member, and a business woman. She was a victim, but now she's a champion. Nora is extraordinary only by her commitment. We have her skills, we have her access, and we have her capacity to understand the problem. Let's now join her and many more like her in the fight against the fatal attraction with alcohol by our youth.

Steps That One Can Take In Confronting the Fatal Attraction

1. Find organizations in your community that fight against underage drinking;
2. Gather data for your community and county. (This material can be acquired through your county substance abuse office and local law enforcement officers. Ask neighbors and other parents to assist.);
   - Number of alcohol-related traffic crashes
   - Number of alcohol-related deaths
   - Number of alcohol establishments per 10,000 population
   - Number of liquor violations in local establishments, including service to minors
   - Underage drinking arrests
3. Find out what policies are in place for bars and liquor stores to prevent sales and service to youth, along with policies related to service of adults who are intoxicated;
4. Find out which establishments in your community create the biggest problem for sales and service to youth;
5. Find out what your school policies are related to underage drinking;
6. Find out what your local colleges and universities are doing to prevent

underage drinking;

7. Contact the Governor's Office to see who administers the Enforcing Underage Drinking Laws initiative in your state. Reach out and volunteer to work with that agency;
8. Listen to your children and their friends when they discuss how alcohol is involved in their lives.

2 - THE POWER OF THE NORM

HIGH SCHOOL NORMS

The high school was like any other....crowds of students meandering through the halls while the sounds of slamming lockers and rushed conversations filled the air as students retrieved books and papers from the metal cubicle that serves as a bedroom away from home. Pictures taped to the inside of locker doors reflected interests and passions that account for how the young men and women spend their time and their lives. Some lockers were neat and clean – others are a reminder of why some parents keep their teenager's bedroom door closed.

I stood in the hall with a teacher as he provided the familiar social breakdown of the cliques and informal clubs that make up most American high schools. The jocks, the skaters, the cowboys, the academics, the thespians, the Goths, the cool kids and the not-so-cool kids – each identified by the clothes they wear, how they talk, where they sit at lunch, and, of course, who they count among their friends. As a former high school teacher and principal myself, I saw nothing different from when I worked in a school. For that matter, I saw very little different from when I was a student in high school many years ago.

Each student I looked at brought to mind someone in my high school class – their attitudes, actions, even physical appearance so similar to young men and women who had been my friends. As I studied their faces, I also recognized the same concerns, doubts, insecurities, and desire to belong that my peers and I once shared. And I watched that familiar ritual of how each hung out with others who had similar appearance and attitudes, talked the same talk, and walked the same walk. Psychologists call this *norming*, the social need that most people have to find refuge and acceptance among those who feel, think, act, and look like they do.

Experts say that norming is the single most influential force in determining your child's decision to drink. Here, in this universal developmental journey, are the seeds of dysfunction around alcohol and the movements toward adults' decisions about alcohol. But, its affect does not end with adolescence. It is also a significant factor in an adult's decision to drink.

On that day and in that particular high school, I was interviewing students about their drinking habits and patterns. I hoped students would candidly report how much they drank, and I was particularly interested in their brand loyalty - what they were drinking and how they had become attached to one brand over another. I had a series of structured interview questions to ask students in this suburban community outside of Cincinnati. I promised the students confidential one-on-ones where the students would be protected against any adverse consequences associated with their alcohol use. I was rewarded with their candor, troubling though it was.

Of 15 students, nine of them had consumed alcohol at least once in the past 30 days. Seven students admitted to having been drunk in the past 30 days, and all seven of those students admitted that they drank only to get drunk. All nine recent drinkers admitted to participating in "risky behavior" while under the influence of alcohol including driving under the influence, having sex, and petty theft. Two admitted to being victims of violence.

There was sadness in their reports. Students whose alcohol consumption led to risky sexual behavior lowered their eyes in shame. "I can't deny that I have been stupid while drunk," said one young lady, laughing nervously. "I wish there was a way I could retrace my steps and get a 'do-over'", another confessed. A male student admitted being overly aggressive with his girlfriend when drunk. "I can hardly look at her now – and she barely speaks to me," he said. "It was, in all honesty, the closest thing to rape that a person could experience." He went on to say, "I am so lucky she didn't tell her parents or for that matter the cops. Dumb! Dumb! Dumb!"

When asked what influences most contributed to their alcohol use, all of them, without exception, admitted peer pressure and the desire to be accepted in an environment where alcohol was being consumed. Of special interest was the students' loyalty to specific brands of alcohol. If they began drinking Budweiser, they were, for the most part, still drinking Budweiser. One articulate and sophisticated student asserted that his initial brand of bourbon was Maker's Mark -- a pricey bourbon popular with young adults. "Only the ignorant drink Jack," a couple said. All of them agreed that advertising helped influence their decision on brand choice.

This conforms to a body of research that suggests brand loyalty is critical to alcohol initiation and long-term alcohol consumption. One area of research that is revealing suggests that much of alcohol advertising directed toward the 21 year-old crowd is about branding. In other words, the alcohol companies clearly intend to communicate, "When you begin drinking – we want you to drink our brand." However, age 21 is not a firm line of demarcation. Advertising that reaches 21-year-olds also reaches 19-year-olds and younger. I can't imagine that it's an accident of marketing that alcohol ads featuring a younger crowd and set in an exciting and adventuresome setting are really about getting the above-21 crowd. None of the high-schoolers had any problem identifying advertising that they felt was funny, appealing, and directed toward them. Furthermore, a key component of the message is about creating a pattern or expectation around behavior; "drinking "our" brand makes you cool or allows you to fit-in with the right crowd."

Community social norms are critical variables in determining when and how young people choose to drink. Many of us remember situations, however awkward they may be, when all around us individuals were drinking, and we were not. There is both indirect and direct pressure to drink or at least an implicit community expectation that drinking would occur. These are a manifestation of social norms, the informal social rules defining acceptable and unacceptable behavior within any social group, organization, or larger social structure, such as a village, small town, or city."[33] Social norms are powerful agents.

Examples of these norms in the alcohol field are widely known and reflect the "culture of alcohol." These norms are the direct result of common beliefs or shared values that are either sanctioned or embraced by a community. You know them and may have even used them in the casual conversations with colleagues, neighbors, or your children.

Can You Recognize These Beliefs?

- Alcohol consumption is a rite of passage for youth; they are entitled to experimentation.
- Most people enjoy alcohol and want it readily available and convenient to purchase.
- Only alcoholics cause alcohol problems, and restrictions on availability have no affect on their drinking.
- Violations of alcohol policy are not a high priority for law enforcement because violators are not major contributors to societal violence and traumas.
- It is acceptable for parents to provide alcohol to their teen-agers and friends so long as they do not allow them to drive.
- Alcohol advertising has little or no impact on consumption among youth and high-risk populations.
- It's nothing to take too seriously. After all, everyone does it.
- I'm hypocritical if I drink and tell my teen-agers that it's off limits for them.
- Having a beer or two on the weekend when I was a kid didn't hurt me, and it's not going to hurt my children.
- Teenagers are going to drink anyway. I'd rather have them doing it in my basement than somewhere else where I can't see what's going on.
- As a parent, I have an obligation to raise my children to be responsible drinkers. How am I

going to do that if I don't allow them to drink while they're still at home?

- If I allow my kids to drink in my presence, they won't sneak off and drink behind my back. They'll talk to me before they go too far or develop into problem drinkers.

Consumer behavior, like other behavior, is affected by the beliefs out of which our cultural and societal values and norms are formed.[34] The high school interviews mirrored that world of the students' social and cultural norms. In their efforts to somehow be individuals, adolescents wind up dressing alike, buying the same brands, styling their hair in common fashion, and making decisions based on a common community norm. One would like to believe that the common community norm about what is right and wrong is defined by some higher moral or ethical principle. Unfortunately, that's pretty rare. Generally speaking, social norms are determined by "group-speak" or what is tolerated by the group. Morality or ethics usually don't come into play.

This kind of moral ambiguity is not isolated among the youth. It dominates our culture, including when and how adults decide to consume alcohol. The first social norm listed above - alcohol is a rite of passage and young people are entitled to experimentation – can undermine everything we do to try to prevent youth consumption of alcohol.

WHEN NORMS GO OFF TO COLLEGE

Jack is an 18-year-old freshman at Becker College in Wooster, Massachusetts. Becker is a dry campus, meaning there is officially no alcohol allowed. Regardless, according to Jack, there is still "a lot, a lot, a lot of drinking" and most people get "really trashed" at least once a week. In an interview with a research associate, Jack's behavioral profile, along with the role of peer pressure and access to alcohol, began to emerge.

Jack grew up in Norwalk, Connecticut, where he and his friends had to rely on older siblings or friends to buy alcohol. Sometimes it was difficult to find someone who was willing, he recalls. At Becker, Jack lives in a dorm full of older students and rarely has a problem finding someone to run to the store. If all else fails, he admits, "I just ask the Resident Assistant assigned to the floor." Jack and his friends, he confessed, usually start a night drinking heavily at the dorm room and then head to a bar or a club. They often go to off-campus house parties, arriving early and staying late. Usually the host of the party charges $5 to $10 per person, and everyone tries to make the most of their contribution by drinking as much as possible.

Jack reported that things got "out of hand" for him at a friend's 19th birthday party. He claimed that the last thing he remembered before passing out was playing a drinking game called Beer Pong.[35] He woke up the next morning in jail. He was able to reconstruct the night from talking to friends and the police officers who arrested him. "I left the party and was walking around with my friends. Someone must have called the cops on us because we were making so much noise, and we were kind of kicking stuff - mailboxes and things. I guess I was arguing with the cops and got loud, so they arrested me. My friends that were with me waited for two hours to try and bail me out, but I was really out of it. The cop said that when he put me in the cell I was walking around like I thought I was somewhere else. I pretended to lock the door, took my pants off, lay down on the cot, and pretended to pull a cover up over me."

Jack faced a number of charges from that night, including disturbing the peace, destruction of property, resisting arrest, and possession of alcohol by a minor. He expected to pay a fine and perform community service. Jack didn't intend to stop drinking. He said that he was not worried about the risk, because if he had only been charged with possession, all he would have to face is a $50 fine. If he ever got caught again, he planned to cooperate with the police and accept his "slap on the wrist." The most telling and sobering aspect of Jack's story was that his drinking was purely social and included plans and strategies to access alcohol and to get drunk. After all, isn't this what one does at college?

Jack's experience points to a number of conflicts in the way community or institutional norms are established around the acceptance of drinking. First, despite attending a dry campus, Jack believed that most people get "really trashed." Second, Jack's fall-back source for purchasing alcohol was his Resident Assistant – an individual who is responsible for enforcing the rules and regulations of the campus. Becker had adopted policies and procedures for preventing youth access or consumption of alcohol. However, the norm for the students at Becker is that these policies and norms are meaningless and can be violated. In fact, there is a reasonable expectation that the Resident Assistant is an accomplice to violating the rules. In short, the behavior of the "village" is what guided and shaped Jack's choices. He made underage purchases of alcohol, he got the necessary help from the over-21 crowd, and he participated in activities that promoted drinking to get drunk. Lastly, but very significant, is his "reality" that he would only face a $50 fine if caught in possession. Those are the norms of his community. Whatever the rules may be, there's no expectation of meaningful enforcement. The norms, in this case, trump the rules.

Norms and expectations are not simply what a community believes or adopts as policy but how a community behaves or is prepared to behave. If everybody believes drinking is a rite of passage and all young people are "entitled" to their time of experimentation, then, kids will drink with impunity. Jack's story included some personal and community consequences, but did the consequences incite reaction by the community's residents? No. After all, what are a few damaged mailboxes and kids making noise late at night? Jack simply wanted to fit into the college scene and be one of the gang. The community basically said, "OK, we can tolerate that."

The Harvard University initiated College Alcohol Study surveyed more than 50,000 students at 120 four-year schools in 40 states in 1993, 1997, 1999, and 2001. The 14-year study shows that the key difference between alcohol-steeped, "wet," and so-called "party schools", and "drier" schools boils down to a simple concept: environment. Students' drinking habits depend to a great degree on the availability of alcohol and their access to it. It has been documented that permitting "tolerance" in these two variables that are heavily influenced by state, college, and community policies, results in far more alcohol related incidents and consequences.

In another interview with a student who attended New York University (NYU), we see how all the above community norms interacted. Laura grew up in a tiny town in the middle of Tennessee. "There wasn't much to do or any place to go," she said. Throughout high school, her friends would sit around and drink beer and whiskey until someone passed out. According to Laura, they did this *every night.*

When Laura moved to attend NYU, she felt out of place and self-conscious. She hated her southern accent and had a hard time thinking of what to say to people who seemed nothing like her. Alcohol helped smooth the edges. When she was drunk, she felt that she was funny and confident. She took to picking up a few six packs of Coors Light Tallboys every night on her way home from class. "Nobody ever asked us for ID," she said. Her roommate Kim did the same, and with alcohol aplenty, their apartment became a natural meeting place for friends. No matter when it was, everyone could always count on Laura and Kim to throw an impromptu party.

Kim was a year ahead of Laura in school. When she graduated and moved out, things started to change. Laura's friends didn't think that her sitting home alone drinking every night was acceptable, not like it had been before when Kim was there. Laura started to drop out of her social circle. She began to spend more and more time by herself. Her financial situation also became difficult, and she was forced to take a job at NYU and attend classes part-time. Soon, she moved to Brooklyn and started frequenting neighborhood bars. She became such a regular at the bar below her apartment that she was often waiting outside for its doors to open at 6 p.m.

Over the next two years, Laura spiraled out of control. She woke up almost every morning with a swig of whiskey and passed out almost every night the same way. She went to bars and talked to anyone who would drink with her, often finding herself in horrific situations in the morning. She gained 30 pounds and couldn't find a way to get healthy again. Even worse, she was so depressed that she didn't have any interest in doing so. She was 23.

Fortunately, and with the help of others, Laura started seeing a therapist and attending Alcoholics Anonymous. Her willingness came when she realized that, if things didn't change, she would soon be dead. Laura had been sober for approximately 11 months when she told us that, "I had to cut myself off from almost everyone I used to spend time with." She said that the problem isn't that "I feel pressure from my old friends to drink, but that I can't put myself in social situations where there is drinking going on." On occasion, she will go to the movies or grab lunch with a friend, but going out at night is a huge challenge. It isn't possible for her to meet up with a group at a bar or a club. Even meeting for dinner is uncomfortable because she hates feeling like she is forcing people to forgo wine or cocktails.

At the age of 24, it is viewed as beyond taboo to be on the wagon. Most people her age think that alcoholism is a problem for older people. She has noticed that even her friends who aren't hard-core drinkers seem to feel uncomfortable. "Going out with them now is hard because I feel like there is still a big neon sign over my head broadcasting the fact that, once again, I don't fit in."

Laura's story speaks to environments, social gatherings, lack of community enforcement around access, and last but not least, the belief that persistent drinking for social acceptance is a harmless activity with no long-term consequences. Laura became an alcoholic. And when that happened, she couldn't fit in with the social norm. It's sad that sobriety can't be the social norm, especially with young people. But it's not.

Laura and Jack reflect a social norm that must be debunked. Popular culture, reinforced by alcohol industry marketing, would have us believe that alcohol is an integral part of American life, that it is a normal accompaniment to almost all social events. The drinking norm would have us believe that most Americans enjoy drinking on a regular basis. These are misperceptions; they're not really true. Most people, including young people, either don't drink or drink only occasionally – and not very much on those occasions. But the perceptions – or rather misperceptions of regular drinking – affect our attitudes toward alcohol and our policies regarding the sale to and consumption of alcohol by youth as well as adults.[36]

DRINKING REALITIES AND SETTING COMMUNITY NORMS

The fact is that, for a large majority of Americans, alcohol is a fairly unimportant consumer product. According to the National Household Survey on Drug Abuse, about 48 percent of adults 21 years of age and older report that they did not consume any alcohol in the past month.[37] Equally important as the frequency of drinking is the quantity people drink on each occasion. "Among adults, 51 percent did not drink at all, and 29 percent drank but did not have five or more drinks on any occasion. That is, 80 percent of adults do not drink at a hazardous level."[38] Let me repeat that again.

- Binge drinkers are 20 percent of the population, but they drink 83 percent of all alcohol consumed.
- Frequent bingers are only 6 percent of the population, but drink 50 percent of the alcohol.

This information is critical to parents, activists, and policy makers. The claim that the overwhelming majority of Americans use alcohol responsibly is true only because most Americans either abstain from or consume alcohol very infrequently. What this also tells us is that segments of the alcohol industry are overwhelmingly dependent upon the Lauras and Jacks of the world because they drink in excess.

Let's look again at the underage drinking population. About 94 percent of 12- to 14-year-olds reported that they had not drunk alcohol, while 75 percent of 15- to- 17 year-olds and 52 percent of 18- to 20-year-olds reported that they had not drunk in the preceding month. In terms of quantity of drinking, the proportion of young drinkers who report drinking heavily (five or more drinks at a sitting) is higher than for adults.

According to research conducted by the Pacific Institute for Research and Evaluation for the Office of Juvenile Justice and Delinquency Prevention, "41 percent of adult drinkers report heavy drinking on one or more occasions in the past month; NOW GET THIS! 51 percent of 12- to 14-year-old drinkers in that 6% who drink, 65 percent of 15- to 17 year-old drinkers in the 25% who drink, and 71 percent of 18- to -20 year-old drinkers in the 48% report very heavy drinking in the past month.

It's clear that the smaller percentage of young people who drink heavily consume the vast majority of the alcohol consumed by their age group (92 percent for 12- to 14-year-olds to 96 percent for 18- to 20-year olds.) Another startling way to look at it is that underage drinkers consume about 12 percent of all the alcohol purchased in the United States, or 3.6 billion drinks annually, and the vast majority of this alcohol is consumed in a risky fashion.

CONCLUSIONS

- The majority of young people abstain from regular use of alcohol – a greater percentage than adults.
- Young people who do consume alcohol are more likely than adults to drink heavily.
- The small proportions of youth who drink heavily consume the vast majority of the alcohol consumed by underage drinkers.

The belief that most adults drink in moderate amounts without any problem translates into public policies that make alcohol readily available at low prices and permit the widespread type of marketing that communicates only positive messages about alcohol's effects.[39] These policies in turn create an environment that encourages alcohol use and downplay its potential for harm to public health and safety. Herein, lays the paradox. Instead of benefiting the responsible drinkers, cheap prices and easy availability make binge drinking and heavy drinking easy. It's not surprising that the alcohol industry likes it that way, because that's where they get most of their profits. Alcohol industry marketing feeds the social norm that heavy alcohol consumption is widespread, particularly among young people. From these perspectives, it's easy to see why.

With these realities in mind, we must begin to design programs, policies, and community projects that shift social norms closer to reality. The way to do this is addressing **the four major influences** that affect the reality of alcohol consumption and youth drinking.

THE BIG FOUR

1. *Alcohol is cheap and becoming cheaper*. In many places, cheap beer is roughly the same prices as popular brands of soft drinks. Cheap booze means more consumption. Kids generally don't have as much money as adults; the cheaper the alcohol, the more they can buy.

2. *Alcohol advertising is a $4 billion dollar part of the industry*. Young people are inundated with media messages that romanticize alcohol and emphasize the "everybody is doing it" message, which is false.

3. *Alcohol is one of the most readily available and profitable consumer products,* a major issue in low-income areas of our communities. Alcohol is often more available than basic staples and school supplies. Alcohol sales are often key to the profitability of convenience stores, markets, and gas stations which may be located in residential areas, near schools, and in other locations frequented by children.

4. *Alcohol products cater to youthful tastes and promote underage and unsafe drinking*. Sweet alcohol products blur the line between alcohol and soft drinks. Malt liquors, which have high alcohol content and low prices, are sold in 40-ounce and other larger containers, which are consumed in one sitting.

I also have talked to students who do not drink. Those who chose not to make alcohol a part of their lives were influenced by other social norms, most of which were religious or familial. Their predominant social influence was their community of faith or the behavior and actions of their parents. In the non-drinkers, there was greater communication and awareness about why underage drinking was a threat to themselves and to their community. Their understanding of alcohol products and intoxication was less informed than their peers even though they might have experienced alcohol-related problems or, perhaps, witnessed them in their past. Nonetheless, these students did not drink and they knew why they did not drink. The "why" was anchored in a personal conviction they had chosen to embrace. Either out of religious conviction, a desire for parental approval, or because they decided not to put themselves in situations of risk or danger, they were not going to drink.

Adrianne is 16 and one of the students from the high school I visited who decided not to drink. She spent considerable time since middle school framing her various responses to the peer pressure she would eventually face. She was quick to point out that most of her friends who drink are not bad people.

Regardless, coming up with honest responses or refusal skills was difficult. She was embarrassed by her commitment. She told me, "I would love to be able to just shout-out that I am not drinking, because I love and follow Jesus. But do you know how stupid I would look if I said that?" Initially she made excuses that seemed to work. She was not feeling well, she would say, or in one case, she told people she had a heart murmur that prevented her from any alcohol consumption. Eventually, she had to move beyond that excuse as she was a statewide champion soccer player. "The good news," she said, "they don't ask as much as they use to." She admitted, though, "I am not sure that I am invited to as many events as I used to be because I think I make them uncomfortable." But, she was unwavering in her convictions: "To change now would make me a big hypocrite."

I was impressed with her resolve. However, as she left the room, she turned to me and said, "You know, I am not sure how I am going to do this when I go to college. I plan to attend Ohio State University, and I want to rush for sorority and enjoy all those things that college can offer. How do you do that and not drink?"

Adrianne looked like her peers, talked like her peers, and shared many of the same values as her peers. In fact, I was struck by the similarity of all the students I interviewed. It was clear that for most students, the social norm was that alcohol was okay, and frankly was a rite of passage. But still, many like Adrianne didn't drink or don't plan to drink in college.

We can build on the common variable in who drinks and who doesn't drink - environment and parental involvement. What can be done to support her? With that in mind, there are things we can do to influence the social norms that govern the choices our children make around alcohol.

CONFRONTING THE FATAL ATTRACTION

Steps One Can Take in Helping Teens Not Drink and Changing Your Community's Norms

1. Hold regular and frequent conversations with your children about community norms and expectations around alcohol. Press them to think about community norms, such as how alcohol is advertised, served at sporting events, found in movies or other entertainment venues. Ask them straight out – what are the pressures and hypocrisies you see about preventing underage drinking?
2. Discuss with your family the formal and informal norms that are seen in your family, neighborhood, and community. How are those norms reinforced? When and how should they be challenged?
3. Engage in discussions about the changing nature of norms. What were the norms for you and your family when you were a

teenager and compare them to the norms of today.

4. If your student applies to a college or university, ask the university about its policies and practices related to alcohol on campus. Ask for written policies, enforcement strategies and the consequences of a student being found in possession of alcohol. These questions should be presented directly to the admissions office or the Office of the President. Ask for any health-related data about alcohol consumption on campus. You are paying their tuition – you have a right to ask these questions and to hold your institutions accountable, especially if they are public institutions.
5. At public events such as festivals, parades, sporting events, hold elected officials accountable for responsible alcohol service; make the case that these are family-oriented events and attention should be given to responsible alcohol consumption.
6. Meet other parents in your children's schools and take steps to communicate consistent messages about alcohol and how it is accessed in the home and in the community.
7. Consult the website wwwbwise.org for more information on strategies to prevent underage drinking on college and university campuses.

3 - THE PROMISE OF FAITH IN BREAKING THE ATTRACTION

I was exhausted from several hours of intense meetings with representatives of the public health community living and working in the Gaza Strip. These meetings were the result of an invitation from the US State Department to travel to the Middle East to consult on the creation of a joint effort to address substance abuse needs in Gaza, now formally a part of the Palestinian Authority. The public health doctors from the United Nations, the Palestinian Authority, and Israel had spent the day peppering me with questions about emerging substance abuse trends in the Middle East. Throughout the day, these dedicated individuals who provide health services in the refugee camps that dot the map of Gaza were alarmed at the increasing number of children and young people using drugs and were especially alarmed at their new access to alcohol. The faith of Abraham in the Middle East has long been a protective factor against substance abuse. Alcohol, however, was now becoming a threat. Westernization and exposure to western media increased awareness and, therefore, demand. These were the issues that dominated our conversations.

The rancor and tension that usually accompanies these meetings between diverse political and religious activists was absent. As soon as the topic turned to the future of their families, their children, and the many threats confronting them, the mood and tone turned to concern, empathy, and compassion.

Our meeting room overlooked the dark wine sea of the Mediterranean providing a vista that was both breathtaking and unsettling. The setting sun on the horizon pulled one's eyes to a spectacular beauty of God's creation while the emerging darkness exposed the pocked marked buildings and stone hewn streets cluttered with rubble, burned tires, and rock from a devastating car bomb the previous day.

The encroaching darkness aroused anxiety in the participants who had to return to their homes before curfew, which signaled to us the need to close. We finished our conversation, and as we were preparing to leave, a Palestinian doctor suggested a closing blessing on our gathering. Fifteen people – Muslims, Jews, and Christians – stood around a table and received a blessing from the God of our faiths. No one questioned the legitimacy of such a blessing, no one doubted the sincerity of the faith of any participant, and no one questioned the need for the blessing. For those in the room – God, Allah, Jehovah – whatever title was appropriate, it was clear that faith was a necessary dynamic for the problems they were facing and solutions they were seeking.

The next day nine of us packed into a minibus and headed for the city of Bethlehem. The van was filled with conversation and stories of their childhood. The jokes and the teasing so common among working professionals filled the air. To get there, we had to clear the security check point or Ersatz that monitored the movement in and out of Gaza. The closer we got to the border separating Gaza from Israel, the more anxious they became, and soon the van was silent. At the check point, armed Israeli soldiers required me and the Israeli members of our group to exit the van and move through a separate line. We were searched and made to carry our bags across a long open area under the watchful eye of armed soldiers. The Palestinians proceeded in the van through a separate line. They waited for us on the other side. The walk across the open area was intimidating and threatening. I felt like I was being punished for traveling with Palestinians and questioned for my association with these dedicated and caring individuals. Suddenly, the unifying blessing from the previous night seemed shattered by the mistrust and hate that divides the peoples of the Middle East. I was angry!

It is the paradox of the region – that the God of Salvation can quickly become the Source of Division, the reason for hate and the reason for mistrust. Man, it would seem, has created a God that can unify and a God that can divide. Yet, over several days of conversation and discussion with these doctors about children's health, it was the children that silenced all division and all mistrust. It was their concern, their compassion, and their protective instinct about children that brought peace and unity to our meetings. At no time in my life have the words of Jesus been more poignant in their meaning and expression: *And an argument arose among them as to which of them was the greatest. But when Jesus perceived the thought of their hearts, he took a child and put him by his side, and said to them, 'Whoever receives this child in my name receives me, and whoever receives me receives him who sent me; for he who is least among you all is the one who is great.'*[40]

The issue of faith and its relationship to how we solve problems and how we view the world remains an issue of some contention among social scientists, psychologists, and public health officials. It is so private and so idiomatic that it is difficult to draw sweeping conclusions across generations, cultures, or nations. Yet, despite attempts to separate faith from the mainstream of our lives, it always resurfaces and demands a response. We may differ on philosophy, theology, and the multitudes of religious beliefs and claims, but it is our faith, regardless of our heritage, that takes us back to core issues of civility, compassion, empathy, and (hopefully) self-control. The child in our midst often appears to define those core claims. In the Abrahamic faiths, to harm a child is to jeopardize one's salvation. I suspect this is true in most traditions.

There is probably no other public health issue that is affected by faith more than the issue of alcohol. Faith and our belief in a "higher power" is so evident in the work of Alcoholics Anonymous (AA) that it would appear that faith is the core ingredient to meaningful and long lasting treatment. Even the Substance Abuse Mental Health Services

Administration (SAMHSA) of the U.S. Department of Health and Human Services publishes material on effective faith-based strategies in treatment. In fact, SAMHSA even goes so far as to state that "The benefits of engaging the faith community in both the prevention and treatment of substance abuse and dependence cannot be overstated."[41]

Joe Califano, formerly at the Center on Addiction and Substance Abuse at Columbia University, has asserted that a young person with a faith foundation is less likely to be involved in crime, violence, or substance abuse. At one level, that is another one of those *NO DUH* statements, yet it is important to emphasize as we think through our solutions to the fatal attraction.

The issue before us is twofold. First, we must understand the role of personal and community faith as both a protective factor in keeping young people off or away from substance abuse, and if addicted, as a way of sustaining recovery. The second component is to understand the role a faith community can have in shaping or defining prevention and intervention programs. Faith-based programs received considerable attention during the Bush Administration, and the Obama Administration promised to keep them engaged. However, there is increased pressure on faith-based initiatives to demonstrate their effectiveness and not totally depend on abstinence as the solution. Faith-based substance abuse prevention and treatment programs should welcome this emphasis. All programs need evaluation.

The active participation of the faith community in shaping and defining programs and services has long been an overlooked strategy for government and funding sources. It is time to welcome them onto the field.

FAITH AS PROTECTION

For Lavonne Harms, personal faith was the defining component of her life, all 17 years of it. Raised in a rural community where religious values were evident in every dimension of one's existence, Lavonne loved her youth group, her Sunday school class, and her church. She was born on a Tuesday, and on Sunday, Lavonne's parents had her in church. She didn't wear her religion on her sleeve, but she was never intimidated by those who did not share her enthusiasm for the gospel. Attractive, extremely intelligent, and well read, every step in her life reflected her desire to serve her savior. She never proselytized nor did she project the "my way or no way" side of some religious enthusiasts. Hers was a quiet faith ready to spring into action when called upon by a need or a question. There was something about her presence that gave peace and comfort to those in her presence. Lavonne faced the same challenges, temptations, and opportunities of any other adolescent female.

We all wish that a strong "parents of faith" model was the dominant force giving support to children. It is the most significant protective factor, but not the only support, for teenagers facing the challenges of substance abuse. The good news is that when parents are not providing or available to provide "faith protection", several groups have stepped up to the plate to provide these services. Consider a couple examples:

Teen Challenge, a faith-based organization with residential addiction recovery centers all over the country, is one example. With its more strident message of the power of God being stronger than the bonds of addiction, their work has been documented as effective.

Though Teen Challenge is often viewed as a strictly evangelistic organization, it does focus on the total person engaging the spiritual (ways to discover God), emotional (healing of past abuses), physical (drug free environment and proper food and exercise), social (tools to work through relationship problems with peers and families at home); and educational (curriculum teaching skills required for them to become successful Christian citizens) aspects. Their adolescent centers provide secondary education and GED programs. The organization uses a 12-month character development program offering a daily regimen of structured and disciplined living.

Robert, of Peoria, Illinois, offers a not uncommon testimony to the success of the program. Now aged 19, Robert started drinking when he was 13. He got involved with a gang, increased his drinking, and started selling drugs. At 17, Robert was kicked out of school and turned to the streets full time. One day, Robert was drinking heavily and doing a drug sale when his friend and girlfriend were killed. In his words, "I got set up for robbery". Robert was accused of the crime and jailed. While incarcerated, he was visited by the local Teen Challenge group who found the resources to clear him of the crime. He committed, upon his release, to become a part of the program. In it, he found help and God. As he testifies, "My faith in God saved me from further destruction. I was trapped in my insecurity; I felt that if I had cars, girls, clothes, and money, I would be happy. But now I know God, and he has blessed me with a beautiful daughter and is molding me daily as a father, husband, and son I want to be."

Overall, Teen Challenge results have been excellent. A study by the National Institute for Drug Abuse found that their centers had an 86 percent cure rate for heroin and alcohol addiction. In 1992, Dr. Roger Thompson of the University of Tennessee at Chattanooga conducted a study focusing on 13 years of Teen Challenge graduates. He found that 75 percent of the graduates were still drug free, 67 percent were abstaining from both drugs and alcohol, and 88 percent needed no further treatment for drug or alcohol abuse.

The Life Process Program at the St. Gregory Retreat Centers offers a very different example of community faith-based treatment of alcohol and drug abuse. Here, a different, spiritually-toned proactive approach is taken to engaging abusers. Rather than presume that an individual is powerless to change behavior, they operate on the assumption that, if given the tools to confront the issues underlying the addictive and dependent behavior, individuals are not only able, but motivated, to change these behaviors. "Tools" include cognitive education, motivational interviewing, and spiritual and life skills training. The strategy is to instill in "students" pathways and skills necessary to move through their addictive behaviors to a life of purpose and positive rewards. The three key components of their recovery program are:

1. A safe, positive, and comfortable environment. They try to make their Center an exciting place to be; not a place to come and dwell on the past or focus on how bad life can be, but to learn how to take back control of one's life. They seek, throughout, to generate hope with facilities designed to encourage that feeling.

2. The emotional and spiritual issues surrounding drug and alcohol abuse are addressed utilizing the skills taught in the program. People are shown how to take with them new tools to confront their problems and make the choices necessary to live productive and successful lives without abusing alcohol. To them, the key advantage of cognitive behavioral training and modification is helping individuals come to their own realizations rather than trying to "convince" them. The net effect to them is that "the consequences of the choice are now real to them."
3. The physical impacts of addiction and alcoholism are addressed through instructional attention to "body damage" caused by abuse, cravings, insomnia, lack of energy, depression, anxiety, and other issues. To address this, individuals are put on a personalized neutraceutical regimen, a natural program utilizing nutrition and specific supplements to aid the detoxifying of the liver and stimulate the proper functioning of the body according to each individual's needs.

Staff primarily consists of educators trained in behavioral modification rather than individual therapists. This process, applied to each individual's life circumstances, serves as a road map for the individual to accurately evaluate problems and work through them in a positive and productive way. Teaching this process and how to apply it to different situations, St. Gregory Retreats maintain that people are able to utilize it for the rest of their lives. Research on results of the approach is hopeful but requiring further study.

These are only two of the many examples of faith-based support given to both protect youth and redeem them from the results of abuse. At the end of this chapter, I've offered some suggestions on how to access current resources or develop your own in serving the community to protect children from abuse.

FAITH AS A FORCE IN SHAPING PROGRAMS

There are some encouraging signs that certain organizations, in and out of government, are responding to the increasing evidence that recovering from substance abuse and addiction is a process that involves the deepest and most complex parts of a person, including the drawing out of the spirituality often hidden or suppressed by addiction.

One such example of governmental and non-profit cooperation to enlist America's Faith Based Community Organizations (FBCO) in an effort to expand recovery opportunities and supportive services for individuals seeking to overcome alcohol and other drug addiction is the federal Faith-Based and Community Initiative which launched the Access to Recovery (ATR) Program in 2003. This program provides approximately $100 million annually in grants that states and some tribal authorities compete to receive every three years. This program of choice among vendors allows clients to choose service providers that can best address their unique challenges enabling them to take greater ownership in their recovery process. Faith-based organizations are welcomed as vital partners in the ATR program.

Many Faith-Based Organizations, operating across the country and committed to the cause, are developing capabilities to address local substance abuse problems by offering, alongside treatment, supportive and caring encouragement to seek a faith that can make the difference for a person trying to break the cycle of addiction. Clients in the program are making wide use of faith based providers. 32 percent of all vouchers redeemed for ATR services by 2007 were at faith-based organizations with an increasing share given to organizations focused on youth alcohol addiction.

The ATR program completed its first three-year grant cycle in 2007. Of the 4,947 organizations participating, more than 1,000 were faith-based nonprofits. Of interest is that nearly 74 percent of clients who were abusing alcohol or other drugs when entering the ATR program were abstinent at discharge, exceeding the success rate of most programs nationally - a high degree of effectiveness. Other studies have been conducted in ATR-funded states including California, Texas, Florida, Missouri, and Connecticut, and the research findings indicate that the ATR program's distinctive approach achieves outcomes that surpass more traditional recovery models.

In September 2007, the second round of ATR grants (ATR II) were awarded as part of its three-year cycle. Twenty-four new ATR grants were competitively awarded to 18 States, five tribal organizations, and the District of Columbia. In the past year, these grantees have enlisted 1,692 organizations as partners to provide services in their community including 580 faith-based organizations. As of October 2008, the ATR II partner organizations have served more than 59,000 clients exceeding the program's goal of serving 35,000 clients with 82 percent of clients abstinent at discharge. More than one quarter (27.3 percent) of the vouchers were redeemed at faith-based organizations. [42]

There is understandably a great deal of due diligence undertaken before requests are awarded, but the main point here is that there is an opportunity for groups organized in an effective way to treat youth alcohol abuse to gain the necessary financing to scale up and be effective with a wider group of clients.

It is hoped that these examples will encourage individuals and organizations to be "bolder" in their advocacy and utilization of strategies to address youth alcohol prevention and abuse in your communities. Now, more than ever, it is needed. And, now, more than before, resources are available to help you make a difference!

As I reflect upon that experience in Gaza where that unity (that three faiths shared around the pressing need to address alcohol abuse) was shattered at the end by the reality of dividing hostilities and mistrust, it was vividly impressed upon me that, if there was a way that we could have somehow insulated ourselves from those pressures - enough to remain united in our common battle against alcohol and drug abuse - we could have seen some real results from those efforts. In a smaller but still significant manner, those of us who are united by faith in this cause must, and can, find ways to put aside our differences and "armor up" against these huge external pressures to make a real difference in our common efforts to eliminate youth alcohol abuse and addiction.

ACTION STEPS

Here are some things you can do to put our common faith to work to make a difference.

1. Understand and internalize the belief that hope and faith are a protection and a strong foundation of resiliency against substance abuse, crime, and violence.
2. Encourage youth involvement in faith-based programs or initiatives.
3. Encourage congregations, synagogues, mosques, and centers of native American

spirituality to actively engage their youth in conversations around the risk behaviors associated with substance abuse.

4. Encourage your spiritual leadership to establish recovery programs in their faith communities.
5. Fund these initiatives and promote active engagement in these organizations.
6. Enlist the help of national faith-based organizations, dedicated to preventing youth drug and alcohol addition, to form such a group in your community, and then support it with your time and resources.
7. Start or become involved in a young mentoring program which exist to provide role models to help youth develop socially and emotionally. Mentors help kids understand and communicate their feelings, relate to their peers, develop relationships with other adults, and stay in school. In the index is a sample of two successful mentoring programs that might serve as starting points.[43][44]
8. Apply as a faith-based group for a government grant to establish a program of intervention in your community. Caution: it can be faith-based but must be non-sectarian.
9. Take leadership in establishing church and off-site educational resources that provide both a knowledge and faith-based case for avoiding alcohol.
10. Provide scholarships to Christian-based outdoor therapeutic programs for youth such as www.mtcarmelyouthranch.com.

4 - FAMILY: BUILDING THE FOUNDATION FOR RIGHT DECISION MAKING

My good friend and colleague at the Pacific Institute for Research and Evaluation, Harold Holder, Ph.D, is one of this country's foremost scholars on alcohol policy. You cannot enter these scholarly waters without encountering the tributaries, and often the rapids, created by Harold Holder. He is prolific and a scientist who has the ability to take complex social policies and translate them into language understood by those of us working in communities. Harold is an engaging and provocative speaker. A lover of outdoor activities, a reader of biography and the classics, he has a presence that reminds you of both an Oxford Don and Grizzly Adams. Regardless, any policy, theory, or strategy being advanced should be examined through Holder's scholarship to be certain that you are not wandering too far down a stream that could eventually leave you high and dry.

Holder begins his important work, *Alcohol and the Community: A Systems Approach to Prevention,* with a dedication that captured my attention and served as a reminder that all alcohol policy begins with family. Holder writes:

> This book is dedicated to my father, Benjamin Solomon Holder, whose earliest teaching to his young son was about the naturalness of the world. I learned the language and concepts of complex adaptive systems later in life, but my appreciation of such systems is rooted in my father's perspective.[45]

Book dedications can be sentimental declarations of gratitude that have little or nothing to do with the substance or content of one's research or writing. And, if one reads' Holder's book closely, you are left wondering what his "father's perspective" actually was. In fact, in some ways that perspective and how it shaped or defined Holder's view of the universe is at least as interesting as the complex systems analysis you find in this seminal work. Our reading of his work may not easily surface a clear understanding or guidance on the role of the family in supporting protection from abuse...or promoting the risk. However, his work on social norms gives us a perspective on the importance of values in shaping our behavior toward alcohol. Those values are anchored in the very foundation of community – the family.

We are all born with one. We may love them, and they may seem to have a Norman Rockwell composition to them. We may not like them, and sometimes they may have the image of the Sopranos or a dysfunctional single parent household. Regardless, family is where we start, and hopefully, it is where we end our journey in life. Most of us, over time, have developed a great tolerance for the behavior and composition of our families. Individual members may embarrass us from time to time. They certainly anger us, and they are an endless source of stories and anecdotes that seem to be told at the most embarrassing moments. Recently, I stood by the bedside of my wife's 98 year-old grandmother as she held my hand in the last moments of her life. She told stories and shared memories of childhood experiences that floated in the air like a butterfly escaping the hold of its chrysalis. These stories seemed to be fleeing a dying and fragile mind and looking to land in the fertile and youthful imaginations of those surrounding her. We laughed with her, we cried, and at times were a little embarrassed by the inappropriateness of the tale –

excused by those of us surrounding her for her dementia and the fact that dying breaks down the boundaries regarding social etiquette. Regardless, I was again reminded that all of us are stitched together by the experiences that begin and end with family.

In the context of alcohol policy and youth access to alcohol, the Century Council, funded by America's Leading Distillers released in 2005 the results of a survey that emphasizes the role of moms in preventing underage drinking. Two results of this survey are worth noting: 1) The conclusion that mothers have a significant role in shaping attitudes about alcohol, and conversely, 2) Mothers are too often clueless when it comes to understanding their daughter's attitudes about alcohol. The most startling finding in the survey is that "nearly half of all mothers think underage drinking is acceptable in different circumstances."[46] The Century Council further summarizes that "mothers of teenage daughters underestimate the occurrence of underage drinking among their own daughters and misjudge the seriousness of the issue."[47]

The data around these findings is quite disturbing. Sixteen percent of 13 to 15 year old girls say they drink with friends. Yet, when their mothers were queried - only 5% thought their daughters were drinking. In the 16 to 18 year old category the disparity between teen use and mother perception was even more striking. Thirty percent of 16 to 18 year old girls say they drink with friends and only 9% of their mothers think they are drinking. There is more consumption in this age group and more denial or ignorance on the part of the parent.

The Century Council Data is even more alarming when it comes to the issue of parental permission or acceptance of alcohol consumption among their daughters. Nearly half (49%) of mothers of teenage girls say it is okay for their daughters to drink. Thirty-eight percent of mothers say it is okay for their daughters to drink on special occasions. Twenty-one percent of mothers have surrendered to the issue of underage drinking, allowing their daughters to drink under parental supervision at home, and 20% of moms basically dismiss the issue by saying it is all part of growing up.[48]

While the survey focuses on moms and daughters, a similar survey of dads and sons would probably be more alarming. Even organizations like the Century Council funds their research in line with substance abuse research organizations like the National Center on Addiction and Substance Abuse at Columbia University (CASA) which stress the importance of family and parents in the prevention of substance abuse. CASA, in a study released in August of 2005, noted the following:

> Twenty-six percent of teens live in households with these four characteristics: (1) frequent family dinners (five to seven times in a typical week), (2) low levels of tension and stress between family members (not very much or none at all), (3) parents who are very or fairly proud of their teen, and (4) a parent in whom the teen can confide. The average substance-abuse risk for such teens is roughly half that of the average teen.[49]

Our colleagues at CASA point to the twenty-six percent of young people who live in homes with these protective factors. They draw a clear correlation between a positive family environment and the prevention of substance abuse. The tragedy is that 74% do not live in this environment. In other words, almost three-quarters of American teens do not have the qualities of a family relationship that

CASA sees as very important for a safe and nurturing environment when it comes to substance abuse.

While parental relationships is only one of several variables for preventing substance abuse or protecting our young people from the harms associated with abuse, it is clearly one of the most important variables. Further, the more consistent and persistent parental involvement and messaging are over time, the more effective that involvement protects children from the harms of alcohol and other abusive substances. And clearly, that involvement must intensify in the later teen years, for as the CASA survey also points out:

> Age remains one of the best predictors of risk: as a teen gets older, his or her substance-abuse risk increases substantially. Twelve-year olds have an average risk score of 0.23—barely a fifth of the average for all respondents (1.00). By the time a respondent reaches age 17, the average substance-abuse risk score increases nearly eightfold, to 1.66.[50]

Family has come to mean many things for this generation. It is the traditional two parent family, it is the single mom, and it is the mixed couple. It is all over the social and relational map. However, and perhaps most significant, family is about having a significant adult in the life of a child. That significant adult, whether related biologically or not, is one of the greatest protective factors in the life of a child.

The relationships we forge over time are complex and diverse. As a teacher, counselor, former minister, and now policy analyst, I have never seen any two families alike. We judge family relationships through the lens of our own experience. I come from a traditional two-parent home with two brothers and two sisters. The reality not seen by my peers and my spouse is that my parents often fought fiercely, separated, and throughout my youth, created an anxiety and fear that to this day, remain a part of my understanding of family. I would visit friends and see what I thought were happier homes, prosperity or wealth, or more familial discourse and be envious of their experience. Yet, I had friends and peers who, being in our home, often wished theirs was as fun and exciting as mine.

Families are bound together by a complex stitching of relational threads that defy easy analysis. They are vulnerable, they are enduring, and they are fragile. However, against the tempest of change, disease, aging, and time, they remain the most defining element of our lives. Memories of good times and bad times, of individual conversations, and of those defining moments of parental instruction that remain a part of my own arsenal of parental advice define who I am. I am from a family, I am part of a family, and I have created a family. Families are the bedrock of our existence. Therefore, we must always begin with that influence and that responsibility.

STRENGTHEN FAMILIES

Every relationship we enter into leaves a marker that influences the way we think or the way we feel about ourselves and our lives. That first relationship is with a mother and father. This relationship begins the very first moments and shapes our responses to the world around us. Much has been written about those moments of birth when an infant enters into the cold harsh world and their senses become inundated by impressions. All that stimuli begins chiseling its way into our bodies and starts the process of shaping our personalities. That process is the sum and substance of both resiliency and risk.

The body of research that has emerged about the importance of family influences is creating many movements dedicated to strengthening families. Strengthening families has also become an important part of the political landscape and is now an integral part of welfare reform and community restoration. There is an acknowledgement by politicians and those funding programs that we must do more to enhance and strengthen families. They are, according to scholars and politicians alike, the foundation of social restoration. Efforts to prevent substance abuse, teen pregnancy, violence, or any other social malady are simply grasping at straws without attention and focus being given to family healing and restoration. While family restoration and strengthening is a difficult and perhaps costly venture for communities, changing policy and environments that endure beyond individual interventions are critical and require family engagement.

Never has it been more important for family strengthening to become an integral part of our efforts to protect our children, particularly our children at risk for substance abuse. Our efforts begin with parenting. It is important to stipulate at the outset that there is no silver bullet or magic formula for right parenting. You can go to bookstores and see endless shelves of books that prod, guide, cajole, and plead with you about how you should parent. I will not add to the list of recommendations or quick fixes but want to stress some principles that might be useful as you think about your role as a parent and how you can also help others to think through their parental roles.

SUPERVISED TIME

Elsewhere, we have acknowledged that, based upon analysis of the National Longitudinal Survey of Youth Behavior, the most important variable in protecting young people from crime, violence, teenage pregnancy, and substance abuse is supervised time. Unsupervised time creates a risk environment that threatens their health and safety. Parental and adult availability in the life of a young person cannot be over emphasized. Children left alone and unsupervised are far more likely to get into trouble than when supervised by an adult.

Because of the economic and social pressures placed on families, it is difficult to have one, much less two parents supervising their children 24 hours a day, seven days a week. However, supervised time need not be restricted to parental presence. How is your child's day structured? Who are the other adults present in that child's life? Based on research conducted by the Office of Juvenile Justice and Delinquency Prevention of the U.S. Department of Justice, incidences of youth crime, violence, and substance abuse are highest between the hours of 3:00 p.m. and 6:00 p.m. This is that critical time when a child has left school and is waiting for a parent or parents to arrive home from work.

While the research is conflicted over the significance of after school activities as a protective factor, there is compelling evidence that when adults are present supervising these activities, young people are less likely to get into trouble. It is important that parents structure their child's activities to include supervision during these times. Also, it would seem important that, as a matter of policy, parents should support community efforts to provide after school activities that have adult supervision.

PARENTS MUST PARENT

Karol L. Kumpfer and Rose Alvarado writing in *American Psychologist* have made the following observation: "The critical role of the family is acknowledged in virtually every psychological theory of child development; however, many parents have given up parenting. They have heard that they have little influence compared with peer and media influences."[51] This statement is especially true when it comes to the critical decision making years between the ages of 14 and 19. Many parents have thrown in the towel. As Johnny and Jane go through their period of adolescent autonomy, parents surrender their responsibilities and do what they can to avoid critical conflict. Wanting to be liked by their teens, they give up parenting responsibilities and negotiate peace through "friendship." It just seems easier that way.

Parents have been told that their influence wanes in this period of a child's development. It is now the peer group and media that dictates or influences behavior. Peer pressure remains the major reason youth initiate negative behaviors according to Kumpfer and Alvarado.[52] However, in a special analysis conducted of the Monitoring the Future survey data, Kumpfer and Alvarado "found that concern about parent disapproval of alcohol and drug use is the primary reason not to use."[53] Parents - this is important to remember. Peers influence initiatory behavior into alcohol and other drugs, but parental disapproval of alcohol and drug use remains the number one reason kids resist peer pressure. This should be a wakeup call to parents who want to surrender this issue to adolescent autonomy. Even at that age, parenting and your approval and disapproval of behavior is still an influence in adolescent decision making. ***Don't Give Up!***

Employing positive communication skills, being present in the life of your child, demonstrating or modeling good behavior, establishing values and expectations are things you should fully engage at this time in the life of your child.

PARENTS SHOULD MODEL BEHAVIOR

Alcohol is a legal product, and many adults consume it regularly in social settings and as a way to disengage, or for some, escape from the activities of the day. Young people can make the distinction between age specific activities. We don't put four year-olds behind the wheel of a car, and we don't permit sixteen year-olds to drink. As a child enters adolescence, they are given more freedoms and responsibilities and most of those are age driven or specific. You need not apologize for your own alcohol consumption, but you need to model behavior demonstrating the responsible use of alcohol.

Modeling behavior begins with your own assessment of how often you drink; how frequently you drink in the presence of your children; how risky your behavior is when you drink such as driving, temper, social interaction, and discourse; and how capable you are of making rational and sound decisions regarding the safety and welfare of your children when you are under the influence of alcohol. These are questions you should ask about your own alcohol consumption and behavior, particularly in the presence of your children.

Most behavioral psychologists would urge you to discuss your alcohol consumption with your adolescents. Don't keep it in the closet or think it does not matter to your youngster. Over time, young people want to know your attitudes and feelings about behavior.

Recently a local newscast featured the stabbing of eight young people at a party in an affluent neighborhood in Northern Virginia. Because of my work and the school environment in which my stepson attends, he is all too aware of my feelings about underage drinking. Regardless, after the report where several neighbors complained about the lack of parental supervision in this particular home, my stepson made the observation or judgment that alcohol was probably involved. I asked, "What makes you say that?" His response was well informed and rational. "You usually don't have that kind of stupidity among teenagers or anybody else for that matter without somebody being drunk and doing something stupid." As the story unfolded the next day in the newspapers, my stepson was right. Alcohol was a factor, and a keg was present in an unsupervised environment.

This incident became a teaching moment. I said to my stepson, "Now you know why I always ask if an adult is going to be present at any party or event you attend outside of our home." "Yea, I get it," he mumbled. He does get it, and he also is quick to affirm that he feels safer in an environment where there are adults providing supervision or guidance.

FAMILY ORGANIZATION AND ORDER

Kids need structure, and the more unstructured their environment, the more chaos breeds, and the more frustrated a parent becomes in their communication. Joseph Califano, Carol Kumpfer, and other family researchers working in substance abuse promote eating dinner together at lease four or five times a week. This is a time for families to discuss concerns, issues, calendars, and topics related to their schooling. While having dinner together as a family may seem like nothing more than symbolism, it represents structured time together and something that should be inviolate in one's schedule. There is an order to such routine that is comforting to a growing adolescent. They can grow comfortable in certain expectations, and they are usually angered or disoriented when that routine is altered. So many of us eat on the run or in front of the television and, consequently, there is no time for conversation or social engagement.

Creating, defining, and enforcing expectations with our children is critical to their success and to their development. In early childhood, we are usually very clear about expectations and consequences if one fails to meet those expectations. When my 20 month-old grandson is playing with a plug near an electrical socket, I can hear his mother communicate very directly about her expectations and his need to change behavior. My hope is that she can find the strength and resolve to communicate just as clearly when he is 16. Household organization and order build confidence and comfort in the life of a child. To be sure, we can get caught in the rut of routine, but I can remember that in a home with order and discipline, how disruptive it was to come home and discover that mom had moved the couch, put the TV in a different corner, and moved dad's chair against a different wall. It felt strange and disruptive. Thankfully, I adjusted.

Organization and order are things we can manage and things we can deliver for our children. We all lead crazy lives and are pulled in a thousand directions, but paying attention to the small things that create order and organization in a home may be the very thing that keeps an adolescent coming home heeding our advice.

VALUES AND EXPECTATIONS

The issue of values is a complex, often risky, but critically important world to enter. There is a cultural war waging over whose values will prevail. There is discomfort whenever we broach the topic, because it suggests that somebody someplace has an answer that transcends generations, gender, culture, and place.

An old sage once suggested that "wherever two or three are gathered together, somebody will always spill their milk." To be sure, when you put individuals together from different families, communities, or a nation, and you will have some stress related to values and social expectations. Somebody is going to say or do something that just does not feel right. They may be small things, or they may be huge issues. In high school and college, I broke up with more than one girl over trivial things such as putting their feet on the dashboard of my car, or when meeting my parents, they failed to respond with yes ma'am or no sir to my parents. One girl broke up with me because she did not like the way I laughed.

While the examples cited above are trivial, they do illustrate that behavior is a window into the soul and value systems of an individual. I like watching how people respond to children, and it tells me something about their values. I remember an elementary teacher, when speaking one-on-one with a child, always knelt down to get eye level with the child. That told me volumes about her view of children and the respect she held for them. I now do the same. Behavior both shapes and emerges from values. Expected behaviors consistently and lovingly applied forge out a value reference. While values are shaped from a number of sources including one's faith, ethnicity, cultural heritage, and country of origin, the primary source of our values rests with our family. Rightly installed, these values will be tested in the communities we live in and in the relationships we forge. Community norms become a yardstick for measuring what is appropriate or not appropriate.

It is, therefore, very important that families discuss openly the values that define their family and their community. What is the "why" behind our choices, decisions, and behaviors? How we act is a mirror of our character. Are we holding a high standard? How many times in our youth did we see the glare of a parent or grandparent when our behavior was an embarrassment or over the edge? That was about expectations and values that defined appropriate and inappropriate behavior. Being clear, consistent, loving, and forgiving are important in shaping the attitudes and behavior of our children.

CIVIC AND SOCIAL ENGAGEMENT

The Corporation for National and Community Service, in collaboration with the U.S. Census Bureau and Independent Sector (a national organization that monitors the work and resources of our nation's foundations) reports that 55 percent of youth volunteer or do community service compared to 29% of adults.[54] That is a big difference and one that is seldom featured on the evening news. In other words, kids are doing some things right. We need to acknowledge and affirm their commitment to service. It has long been understood in the crime prevention community that, the more young people are engaged in community service activities or assume ownership of programs or activities that restore neighborhoods, the less likely they will be involved in destroying those communities. Giving at-risk youth the opportunity to build, create, and restore property or lives keeps them out of trouble and part of a community solution.

Years ago, I ran a summer youth academy for at-risk youth. We had at-risk middle school students serve as tutors and coaches for at-risk elementary school students. Students spent a half day on academics and the remainder of the day in sports or other skill development activities. If the middle school student could add 2+2=4, they were a tutor. We watched troubled kids turn into problem solvers and caring individuals as they nurtured and coached their young protégés. The transformation was palpable.

Families can encourage and promote civic engagement and voluntary service by helping their children think about the needs and concerns of others. They can structure activities where the family is working together in a volunteer environment. An example is the suggestion by former First Lady, Laura Bush that families should consider donating one of their mini-vacations to hurricane reconstruction in the South. Take the money, the time, and the energy of the vacation and do volunteer work with any number of organizations or faith-based agencies rebuilding Louisiana or Mississippi. The lessons learned on these family excursions, with a focus on helping one's neighbor, will make a lasting impression on your child. I assure you, young people involved in these types of activities are less likely to be involved in substance abuse, crime, or violence. Furthermore, we now know "that a youth from a family where at least one parent volunteers is almost twice as likely to volunteer than a youth with no family members who volunteer – and nearly three times as likely to volunteer on a regular basis."[55]

Understanding the role of family and how family defines and shapes our actions is every bit as important as the most sophisticated policy solution we can offer. Systems, policy initiatives, and age-specific programs contribute to preventing underage drinking. However, the behavior, the messages, and the coaching a parent can offer is the contribution that is usually remembered throughout one's life.

Breaking the Attraction Through Family: Actions For Parents And Communities

1. Communicate clear values and expectations around alcohol.
2. Strongly discourage the use of actual or near "imitation liquors" such as Fentimans Victorian Lemonade or Mike's Hard Lemonade which creates a taste for more alcohol under the guise of "coolness".
3. Be open about responsible use of alcohol (particularly your own).
4. Take a parenting class around teen parenting which can be valuable and can help strengthen your family.
5. Organize your home and provide a sense of security that reflects consistency and normalcy.
6. Eat dinner as a family and yes - how about turning off the TV.
7. Promote family friendly work environments. Encourage employers to provide leave for school conferences and extra-curricular activities.
8. With children and all family members, clearly and consistently COMMUNICATE, COMMUNICATE, AND THEN COMMUNICATE. Use teen friendly websites such as www.coolspot.gov as a discussion guide.
9. Discuss with your neighbors and friends the importance of knowing where your children

are at all times and band together to secure that awareness.

10. Encourage your children to have back-up call centers so if you can't find them or they can't find you – there is another place to contact.
11. Discuss with other parents the dangers or concerns regarding the social hosting of parties where parents feel it safer to provide alcohol. Engage this conversation around the health issues, the legal issues, and the issues of liability.
12. Promote, participate, and encourage civic engagement and volunteerism with your children.

5 - THE POLITICS BEHIND THE ATTRACTION

The explosion of gunshots startled us. We reacted on instinct. We had not seen the car coming until it had sped around us, slowing down some 200 yards ahead and opening fire in a neighborhood that was trying to enjoy one of the first warm nights of the season. I was riding with the Wichita Police Department Gang Unit and watched in horror as a young man fell limp in front of a house where children, once playing, were now running for cover. There was not enough time to get the license plate number of the shooters' car before it fled in the smoke of burning rubber and squealing tires.

Brad Carey of the Wichita Police Department Gang Unit began pursuit stopping long enough to let his partner (Kent Bauman) and me out of the cruiser to assess the condition of the victim. As I knelt by the young victim's side, I glanced up at the faces of the children who, with the shooters' car now gone, were beginning to gather around us, curious but surprisingly calm. The sound of a siren grew into the distance and then was joined by other sirens as additional squad cars joined Officer Carey in his pursuit.

The grass was already soaked with blood from a chest and head wound. Trying to determine the condition of the young man, I studied his eyes. They were fixed on me. Filled with horror, I leaned into him providing as much comfort as I could while we waited for the emergency medical technicians to arrive. Again, I looked at the faces of the curious children and wondered if the violence would ever end and how many more lives it would claim before it was over. Then the boy squeezed my hand. I looked down and heard his last words: "Help me." My khaki pants were soaked in blood. My other hand, which I had placed on his head, was covered with pieces of scull. As he died, I fell back just as his mother came running to his side. "No. No. Oh, no," she screamed, falling to her knees and doing the only thing she could: cradle her dead son in her arms. This event was a major intersection in my life, and it greatly influenced how I would spend my time and energy for the next several years. I have thought about this event almost daily. While it took place nearly 20 years ago, it is etched in my conscience. I think of it often, particularly as I meet with the staff of members of Congress and the members of Congress themselves. What I think about may seem strange, but in the battle for dollars and reasonable and responsive policy where politics is so much a part of the struggle, I think about that young man and his mother and the fact that at no time did the family ask me if I was a Republican or Democrat. They just asked for help.

Three months ago, while visiting a hospital in Baltimore, I made my way to the neo-natal unit of one of the nation's premier hospitals. The ward had four babies going through the horrors and pains of cocaine and alcohol withdrawal. They were crack babies also born into the world of Fetal Alcohol Syndrome (FAS). I watched as the nurses and volunteers tended to the infants; most were low birth weight and suffering from tremors as their bodies separated themselves from the drugs and alcohol ingested by their mothers. All four of these children would survive, but the long term learning disabilities and damage would take years to diagnose and overcome. They would soon return to environments that would threaten their survival. I visited with two of the mothers who were struggling with their addiction and feeling the guilt and shame of what they had done or were doing to their newborn infants. Their lips were parched and their eyes were sunken. They had faces of despair and anger. Neither of the women had seen a doctor in over six months. They knew that their actions were jeopardizing the health of their children, and they did not want or need a lecture from a public health doctor who viewed them as part of a large warehouse of clients that were caught in the cycle of urban drug abuse.

We discussed many things. We talked about jobs, the resiliency of youth, education backgrounds, when and where they first started their drug use, their goals, and their dreams for their children. We talked about their neighborhoods, how easy it was for them as teenagers to get access to alcohol, and how on every corner there was a crack and meth dealer waiting to ply their trade. They were in constant pursuit of an anesthetic that would numb their senses to the world around them. When drugs were not available, alcohol was always there. One mother was 17 and the other was 19. As we talked, we discussed their lives, their history, and their hopes for solutions. At no time did we discuss whether they voted for George Bush or John Kerry.

At no time did we discuss the politics of the Maryland General Assembly. The Mayor's name never came up nor did they know the name of the Chief of Police.

A gang member and alcohol addicted mothers of crack babies all were desperate for help and escape. In the media images and the political and policy discourse that dominates our legislative halls, where it appears that often the egos and agendas of elected officials and celebrity spokespeople are in constant need of massaging, nobody seems to see the individual. The victims of violence, substance abuse, and poverty have become the road kill on our journey to pave a moral universe that wants to ignore the pain and sufferings of our neighbors, our children, and our citizens.

The politics of substance abuse is every bit as intriguing, disgusting, and fueled by the mother's milk of all politics - money - as any other field or interest of the public. Most of us working in advocacy or public health are tentative about our relationship with elected officials. Yet, it is often the lobby with the most dollars that greases the wheel that grinds out public policy. Advocacy groups and parents are often left on the outside begging for attention when it comes to shaping alcohol policy. It is hard to compete with organizations like the National Beer Wholesalers Association who annually flood the Hill with their members wearing badges that read "Beer: American's Drink". We cannot surrender this ground to that voice.

It is imperative that the life and death issues that confront a society be elevated above the partisanship that defines many of our decisions. If we are to succeed, we must transcend this partisanship and expose this as an issue that threatens a nation. Therefore, we must find a way to confront the politics, and if necessary, use the politics to advance our mission.

MISSION vs. SELF-INTEREST

The movie Jerry McGuire, the sports agent portrayed by Tom Cruise, is well known for a number of compelling and provocative movie lines that have found their way into mainstream culture. Not the least of which are the lines, "Show Me the Money" and "You had me at hello", and of course, "You complete me." I like those lines, and as someone who likes to raise money, I assure you I have used, "Show me the Money."

Often lost in the discussion of Jerry McGuire is the famous Mission Statement or position paper drafted after a spasm of conscience. The paper challenged the foundations of his career choice trying to negotiate signing deals for athletes who were seeking millions in signing bonuses, contracts, and endorsement deals. The viewer never actually gets to hear or read the mission statement, but it is clear that the document is an iconoclastic attack on the foundations of his industry. McGuire saw the absurdity of a culture willing to pay millions to watch individuals run down a field or put a ball into a hole. He questioned the very foundation of his existence and decided to distribute the Mission Statement to his colleagues and clients. Big mistake! We now know the consequence - he was fired for speaking his conscience. The ingénue of the film, Rene Zelwegger, quits her position in the same firm and leaves with Jerry because she is so taken by an individual with a mission, much less a mission statement. They leave together and set up their own firm. Jerry wants to forget the mission statement, but she won't let him. It continues to play havoc in his life and forces him into a number of decisions that authenticates his existence and defines his future.

We must find the Jerry McGuires in politics. We need politicians who have maintained their convictions and have had the courage to talk about it. We could all benefit by public mission statements.

To be sure, most elected officials have made enormous sacrifices to serve in their positions. I genuinely believe that they seek to do the "right thing". They are pulled in so many different directions and are offered so many different alternatives. We must find these leaders and find ways to support their courage and provide the intellectual and social capital they need to advocate for our children's health and safety.

You can meet with all 435 members of the House of Representatives and all 100 members of the Senate, and to the person, they will tell you that they are opposed to any practice or policy that encourages or promotes underage drinking. They will show up at rallies and events on the Mall celebrating the 25th anniversary of the raising of the drinking age to 21, and they will go to schools and provide personal counsel and stories that would encourage or inspire young people not to drink. Then, you begin to see how easily they are seduced by the clever arguments of an industry that seeks to promote the legal and rational consumption of alcohol.

A classical example or illustration of the conflict is found around the issue of taxes and the price of alcohol. The alcohol industry has been fighting for the repeal of the excise tax on beer since the beginning of the Civil War. It was during the Civil War that taxes were placed on luxury items and alcohol to help finance the War. These elected officials reasoned that, since many of the luxury tax items had been repealed, it was time to repeal the tax on alcohol. The argument made by the alcohol industry was that such increases in taxes cost jobs in the alcohol industry. According to one Senator's office, there are 41,000 jobs in his state related to brewing, wholesaling, and retail. The industry directly and indirectly accounts for close to 2.5 million jobs nationwide. "A reduction of the beer tax would help brewers maintain or grow this workforce," said the release.

This came out of the mouth of Senators who seek the favor of the religious right and promote and champion values-based education and faith-based strategies to minister to the needs of the poor and disenfranchised. Most of the religious right in their states promote abstinence and would certainly take a strong moral stand on alcohol promotion to young people. Most evangelical and fundamentalist religious groups flowered in the culture of prohibition; and the likes of Carrie Nation closing down taverns and saloons in the 19th Century were the heroes and heroines of the abstinence proponents. Yet, this senator seems conflicted when it comes to raising taxes on this product. What does this have to do with taxes? Let me be clear. The price of alcohol has impact on youth access. Clear evidence from research indicates that raising alcohol taxes is one of the most effective measures for reducing alcohol-related problems particularly among young people. Conversely, alcohol policies that foster increased consumption, (e.g., extended hours of sale), tend to have negative consequences for public health.

Proposals to expand alcohol availability as an alternative means of increasing state tax revenues are at odds with research findings and detrimental to public health. Such proposals do not serve the objective of reducing deficits. Revenues may increase, but public health, law enforcement, and other costs also rise. Raising alcohol taxes, on the other hand, increases revenues and at the same time reduces public expenses.[56]

Alcohol prices have not kept pace with inflation, and thus, the real price of alcohol has been dropping steadily. Many different studies have found that higher alcohol prices lead to lower consumption and fewer alcohol-related problems. Higher prices tend to have a particularly strong effect on young people. The higher the prices the less access by youth and by the problem drinker. Advocates have long suggested that the taxes on alcohol should be high to discourage access and to also help fund programs aimed at treating the problems caused by illegal or inappropriate use. The data on this point is clear.[57]

I am going to assume that many prominent United States Senators and their staff have not seen this data. Otherwise, I think, given their moral foundation or spiritual base, that they would seriously examine the consequences created by lowering the tax on beer. A senator who claimed that high taxes threatened 41,000 jobs in their state last year failed to note that there were over 250 underage drinking deaths. How much does a life cost?

On another occasion, a staff member of a prominent U.S. Member of Congress told me that her boss did not have time to participate in an underage drinking caucus. I asked if that member of Congress would be willing to talk to the mother of the last child killed in a traffic accident because of alcohol. The staff member resented my question and suggested that I did not understand the competing interests that challenged her boss. "No," I said, "your boss may not understand the seriousness of this issue or he would certainly make this a priority of time and resources." Fortunately, this is only one member. Many others have expressed more than a willingness to help create and join such a caucus. These members are to be celebrated.

Without a doubt there exists the political "wink and nod" of underage drinking prevention in Washington and in most political circles. Before the cameras and media, a significant number of elected officials are quick to stand shoulder to shoulder with public health advocates and parents. However, they are also quick to endorse the efforts of an industry that contributes significant dollars to their campaigns. It is amazing to watch. One week there will be a press release on the horrors of underage drinking and the next week a press release on lowering the beer tax. Public Health and Youth-Based Advocacy Groups cannot compete with the private sector when it comes to campaign contributions or influence. I use to tell members of Community Anti-Drug Coalitions of America (CADCA) that the reason the Beer Wholesalers win the legislative battles is that their membership gladly pays $2,000 a year in membership fees, and CADCA members complain about membership dues at $200 a year. It is no wonder they win the field.

The fact is, we may never have the resources that the alcohol industry representatives have nor can we compete with their political influence; however, we can be smart - if not smarter than - the opposition. The weight of our arguments and the content of our message have a moral and political influence that is compelling to the public and to the media. We need to continue to advance good science and solid research and position ourselves before the public in a way that compels a response.

DEVELOPING A STRATEGY

Let's begin by putting the situation we face into perspective. It is not fair to paint the entire industry with the same brush. Not all segments of the alcohol industry act in irresponsible ways. There are promising practices emerging out of the alcohol industry that merit attention and support.

Unfortunately, most public health organizations have elected not to have conversations with the alcohol industry because they appear to be the enemy and the source of most of our problems. That is a mistake, and it is based on faulty assumptions.

1. There is the assumption that the industry is monolithic and defined as one element or force.
2. There is the assumption that they all want to prey on our youth. After all, 20% of alcohol profits are the result of underage drinking or consumption. They don't want to lose that market share.

Assumption One

The alcohol industry in this country is highly competitive and structured around a three-tiered system institutionalized in the repeal of the Volsted Act in 1932. There are producers, distributors, and retailers. The three tiers are designed to eliminate monopolies and avoid any collusion that would give any one sector too much control. The large beer producers in this country are Anheuser-Busch, Coors, and Miller. All three have recently been bought by global companies. However, they still control about 52% of the market share of beer world-wide. They remain the most intimidating force in beer production. In the world of distilled spirits, Diageo and Pernod Ricard are the largest producers. These companies are London-based and French-owned, respectively. Together, they control about 70% of market share. The Distilled Spirits Industry of the United States (DISCUS) is the industry association representing the political and commercial interests of the spirits industry. The Wine producers are highly idiosyncratic and diverse. Market share is split among numerous producers.

The distributors and/or wholesalers get the product to the retailer. They are a formidable force in local communities. They want as many outlets as they can possibly accumulate. They work to protect the retailer, and the producers must usually bow to the whims and dictates of the wholesaler. The Beer Wholesalers of America and the Wine and Spirits Wholesalers are the associations that represent the wholesale industry.

The retail tier or sector is probably the most complex of the three tiers. The retailers are state-controlled stores (alcohol control systems in 18 states); private retail outlets (in the remaining states); grocery stores (mostly beer and wine); on-premise serving areas such as restaurants, taverns, and bars; and finally, convenience stores (also beer and wine). In the venues such as restaurants and convenience stores, 35 to 40 percent of their profits are based on the sale of alcohol. Because of that profit margin, these industries fight to protect access. They also are the ones that often have the most to lose if they are out of compliance with liquor control boards. Their license is suspended or revoked; they feel significant economic pain. In the retail sector, one cannot ignore the sale of alcohol at sporting events, concerts, and other large community venues. These events are perhaps the most difficult to control, and they have a lot to lose if they are caught selling to minors. The Toronto Maple Leafs had their FC Stadiums' alcohol licenses suspended for three major league soccer games and lost over $600,000 in revenue.[58]

It is a mistake, as we mentioned before, to see these tiers as one industry. They are often engaged in internecine wars, undercutting practices, and hostile legal battles over reforming or repealing the three-tiered system. Because of these realities, community coalitions, activists, and public health must learn to approach these systems differently. Each of the sectors find themselves involved in community prevention efforts and want to be seen as promoting practices and policies that prevent underage drinking. But how they promote practices and policies are very different. Producers, for the most part, have the luxury of advancing policies that sometimes put them in conflict with the retailer.

The tension between wholesaler and retailer and the policies that dictate or guide their marketing has been made more complicated as large warehouse stores, such as COSTCO or SAMS CLUB, have entered the market as a retailer but often behave like a wholesaler. They seek the price advantage of purchasing directly from the producer. These stores, as with their other products, seek the price advantage of purchasing in large volume and then having the capacity to lower the price to individual consumers. We have already discussed the public health consequence of cheap booze, but more important is the threat to the three-tiered system that monitors monopoly or market share. This debate played out most recently in the courts in Washington State where COSTCO defined themselves as both wholesaler and retailer and sought to purchase directly from the producer. This is still being played out in the courts, but community advocates and parents should pay attention to this issue because it will have a direct impact on price and access to alcohol.

Assumption Two

It is easy to imagine that the alcohol industry wants nothing to do with any effort to reduce youth access to alcohol. Again, youth consumption of alcohol accounts for about 11% of all alcohol consumed and accounts for 20% of the profit made by the alcohol industry. Why would they want to stop this rather significant stream of revenue? The usual answer to this question by public health skeptics and folks accustomed to working with the various tiers of this industry is that they don't want to do anything that threatens that revenue stream. Not true! Alcohol has watched closely the costly and heated debate around tobacco.

The $250 billion tobacco settlement and the public relations nightmare created by the legal wrangling that contributed to the settlement has more than caught the attention of the alcohol industry. They are hearing messages from the Attorneys General of the various states that, in many ways, alcohol practices are worse than tobacco. Could they be the next target of a class action suit, or worse, undergo the PR debacle faced by tobacco? This question has taken the alcohol industry down some interesting paths of collaboration with public health. I think we should begin to take the industry at its word – that they want to stop underage access to their products. If we could begin our conversations with that assumption, then perhaps we can find common ground and begin working together on strategies to prevent youth access.

I believe that some of the following strategies can be carefully discussed with all three tiers involved in the industry with the objective of forging a collaborative approach supported by the combined resources of the alcohol industry and respected community groups or opinion makers.

- Advocate for a comprehensive set of state minimum drinking-age laws that include possession, sale, and age of employees at outlets
- Create a coalition for stronger enforcements of these laws (i.e. through identification checks, keg registrations, etc.)
- Create a strategy for limiting the number of alcohol outlets, particularly in neighborhoods disproportionately affected by crime, violence, and drug abuse
- Advocate for the creation of laws controlling high-volume sales (i.e. drinks served in pitchers, fish bowls, buckets, etc; or limits on happy hours)
- Agree to limits on questionable marketing practices such as 25 cent

beers, all-you-can-drink specials, and "ladies night" when women drink for free or greatly reduced prices.

The discussion should center around how to take the high road by changing the environment in which people drink.

Whatever has motivated them - the threat of a lawsuit, public relations, or genuine concern - let's seize the moment and take the conversation into their house and find out just how serious they are. The only groups that will or should have trouble with this strategy are the prohibitionists. Serious prohibitionists cannot have conversations with an industry they believe to be the root of all evil, or at least all substance use and abuse. However, those of us who see prohibition as a failed social policy and acknowledge that alcohol is a very real part of the daily commerce of our culture, need to help the industry identify problems and then problem solve together in order to assure the health and safety of our community. This strategy is one that not only applies to underage drinking but all forms of problem drinking. It is difficult if not impossible to change the behavior of an individual, a community, or a business if you do not actively engage them in conversation around the problem behavior. Marginalizing the industry in discussions around prevention of underage drinking or problem drinking will make our problem worse – not better.

What Are Those Areas of Common Ground?

1. Jointly communicating the risks associated with alcohol consumption, particularly over consumption;
2. Communicating the dangers and health consequences of binge drinking;
3. Providing interventions at the point of sale in order to break the backbone of the fake ID industry;
4. Working together to address alcohol promotions on the college campus that apply strategies that encourage youth consumption;
5. Acknowledging that there is a problem related to alcohol advertising and that alcohol advertising (both in exposure and content) is penetrating the youth market;
6. Collaborating with community groups to regulate the number of alcohol outlets in neighborhoods disproportionately affected by crime and violence;

7. Acknowledging that the alcohol industry has developed some pretty sophisticated communications tools that speak to youth consumption of alcohol; or in other words, use their material;
8. Standing shoulder-to-shoulder with industry groups before legislative bodies advocating for mutually agreed upon messages and policies;
9. Encouraging your national membership organizations to engage in conversations with the major producers to develop a prevention and intervention policy strategy that can be advanced by Congress and state legislatures;
10. Developing joint policy briefs and materials that can be used by community-based organizations to promote prevention;
11. Holding joint press events to call attention to the harms associated with underage drinking.

These represent a few of the strategies that beg for collaboration or communication. In some ways these are easy. The one issue that remains to be addressed and is fraught with all kinds of controversy and opinion is the issue of money. Somehow, it always comes down to money. They have it, we don't. They often want to give it to us, but we don't take it for fear that we will be compromised in our efforts.

If the various components of the industry make money, so what? If they use that money to prevent youth access, then we should find ways to support those efforts.

Over 3,212 lives depend on us thinking outside the box. If the industry provides resources to communicate a harm message and it saves a life, then I am not going to complain. When, not if, the industry crosses the line on policy or promotion, we should be in their face with every ounce of strength we can muster. If they don't like it, they can keep their money, and we will be glad to communicate that hypocrisy to any and all media. I don't think the alcohol industry is there any more – again remember tobacco!

EXAMPLE OF AN INNOVATIVE STRATEGY

In the past, my organization advanced legislation aimed at breaking the backbone of the fake ID industry, a $75 billion a year industry that continues to facilitate youth access to alcohol at the retail level. The legislation would provide relief and an affirmative defense for retailers who use technology designed to scan and validate government issued identification documents. In other words, if they use the technology, they are held harmless for civil or criminal liability in the event of a law suit. A $500 purchase of this technology could save the retailer millions in punitive or liability judgments for selling to a minor. The legislation has a strong enforcement component aimed at enhancing law enforcement compliance checks and to monitor the behavior of retailers, particularly those with questionable ethics around such sales. In short, the legislation is designed to protect the good retailer and punish the bad retailer. This makes good business sense. I don't care how you slice it. Many retailers, particularly those from American Beverage Institute, claim that the bill is a Trojan horse aimed at strengthening enforcement and catching those restaurants or retailers not in compliance or selling to a minor. In meetings with the industry, I always begin by asking if the industry truly wants to stop youth access to alcohol. To the group they all answer, "Yes." Yet, they are intimidated or frightened by a strategy that would provide tools and enhance enforcement. Funny, the highly ethical retailer has nothing to worry about from enhanced enforcement. The "bad" retailer does, and he/she should be caught and driven out of business. They are breaking the law and threatening the lives of our children. Further, it is these corrupted retailers who create an unfair market advantage for their businesses by employing tactics that promote profits from an illegal and underage consumer. Because of this competitive pressure, the responsible retailer eventually feels the pressure to also "wink and nod" on applying the law.

This legislative effort had industry support but ultimately failed because organizations such as the American Beverage Institute convinced members of Congress that this would add costs to their members (restaurants and taverns). This industry already has a narrow profit margin and enforcing these strategies would, according to them, further reduce those profit margins. What they fail to realize and don't communicate to their members is that, increasingly, states are adopting "Source Laws" that allow the state and victim to sue the provider of alcohol in the event of an injury or death caused by over consumption. The Retail Assistance Act would have provided them a reasonable and defensible cover.

RECONCILING THE POLITICS

Much has been made of the contradictions and conflicts in the political arena. Often the behavior of a profit-driven industry and a political-driven legislative body fly in the face of our goals and objectives to prevent youth access to alcohol. On the other hand, I am always pleasantly surprised when I see courage or conviction supersede personal or private interest. The battle to get states to adopt .08 as the maximum level of blood alcohol content for operating a motor vehicle or for a legal definition of intoxicated is a great example of industry support of reasonable policy. Now a national policy, it was finally made possible when Diageo, the world's largest producer of alcohol, adopted .08 as a policy they could and would support. We should applaud Diageo for having led industry interests in supporting .08 legislation in all states. They were threatened and intimidated by certain retailers, but they held their ground and prevailed. Again, Beam Global, working in collaboration with State Attorneys General, voluntarily lowered their advertising exposure threshold from 25% to 15% because they recognized that their advertising has impact on behavior. This decision was done in conversation with prevention advocates and the traditional substance abuse watch dogs that monitor industry behavior. These are but a few examples of profiles in courage that speak to conviction vs. profit or self-interest.

Outrageous choices on the part of political leaders and/or industry representatives, while seldom done solely behind closed doors, gain momentum when a disinterested or apathetic public do not engage them or hold them accountable. Further, we should never assume that industry or political leadership have heard our voice or understood our position. I cannot tell you how many times a legislator or industry representative has thanked me for both listening and communicating on our issues. More often than not, it is about communication. Especially with political leadership, you have the right to access and you have the responsibility to communicate openly and honestly. They may have competing interests, but as a voter, you are their interest.

Politics on this issue are inevitable. There are so many interests and so much money at stake. Yet, we must stay focused on the mission. There is a biblical admonition, "by all means – save some."

The "all means" can be troubling at times, and it points to contradictions in our strategies and in our lives. Yet, to save all or to save some, we must be prepared to go into environments that threaten to contaminate or do harm. In two of the three stories that opened this chapter, I was in a place that I would not normally be. Had I not been there, my understanding of the issues would have been partial and my capacity to offer assistance significantly altered.

The carnage associated with underage alcohol consumption will not go away without all parties engaging the issue at the most basic level – community involvement. It is in the community that the retailer is most affected by community outrage; it is in the community that elected leaders are most threatened by community input. Building community capacity and moving individual agendas to support a common mission should be a priority for individuals and organizations. Therefore, we must take our message to that most basic and fundamental unit of our communication – where citizens live and work daily – the community.

Action Steps: Things That Parents and Communities Can Do

1. Meet with elected officials (local, state, and federal) to clearly identify your priorities around underage drinking;
2. Call and write letters to your Congressional Delegation; Letters matter and they respond to both message and number of letters;
3. Attend town meetings held by candidates and always ask the relevant questions about what they are going to do about underage drinking;
4. Invite elected officials to attend Victim-Witness panels (panels where victims of drunk driving communicate the horrors of their experience);
5. Publish voting records of elected officials on the alcohol issue;
6. Track campaign contributions and publish the results. Monitor industry contributions to candidates running for office;
7. Meet with representatives of the various tiers of the alcohol industry and explore common ground for cooperation and collaboration;
8. Invite the industry to meet with the media and editorial boards to discuss the common ground between public health and the alcohol industry;
9. Give industry credit when it is supportive of our mission to prevent youth access to alcohol;

10. Share holding in the alcohol industry creates opportunities to influence industry policy;
11. Work with the industry to achieve voluntary compliance to outlet distribution, hours of operation, and Sunday sales issues;
12. Do NOT DO THIS ALONE! Get other parents and community-based organizations to assist in this strategy. You are stronger in mass numbers.

6 - RESPONDING NOW TO THE CALL TO ACTION

I applaud the number of people who immediately, actively, and continuously work to stop teen alcohol use, advocate for constructive changes in the age limit laws, and push in other ways for a better approach to prevent teen drinking. Why? Because, if you are doing this, you are part of a dedicated minority. In spite of the many sources of literature and research documenting the consequences of abuse and the need for increased enforcement and the call from many quarters to "get involved", the fact is that most well meaning people do not respond. One would think that the significant numbers of people impacted by the pain and consequences of youth alcohol abuse would be highly motivated to find a way to enlist and join with others to attack the problem and insist on changes in policies, laws and behaviors that would prevent more damages and consequences to kid's lives. It hasn't generally happened. Why?

I don't think it's because of intentional callousness but rather to a host of other reasons. One reason, emphasized in chapter one, is that alcohol use among especially older teens has been historically engrained in our culture leading many people, including parents, to rationalize that this behavior is part of the "rite of passage" in which young people are view as entitled to their "experimentation". That position, added to the industry's continuous promotion of alcohol as a desirable and important part of the good life, has softened peoples' mindset and will inhibit many who might have otherwise been sufficiently aroused to promote change and engage in activities that could make a real difference.

Other reasons for the initiative may not be that apparent to those who think superficially about the issues. Take the contribution of young students and workers to the $135 billion dollars annually dropped in lost productivity, one consequence of drinking focused on in a recent Robert Wood Johnson Foundation study Those who see this staggering amount may be initially shocked but fail to probe the details and see that youth alcoholism is a key contributor to that statistic. The National Alcohol and Drug Abuse Treatment Rehab Help Information Center estimates that 17.4% of the amount of lost productivity is due to the absenteeism and negligence of young workers between the ages of 15 and 25. If that important detail were highlighted, it might make some difference in the level and rate of response to the problem.

Another "hidden" fact that otherwise might motivate more action are the findings of neuroscientists regarding the potentially permanent effects of teen drinking on brain development. Current and emerging research studies are concluding that, before the age of 21, not only is a young person's brain sufficiently undeveloped to comprehend mortality, consequences, and liability of actions, but excessive drug and alcohol use can retard or permanently damage that full capability. In a study published in April, 2009, researchers from San Diego reported that young people who binge drink can seriously damage the white matter in their brain, which is crucial for relaying information between brain cells.[59] Researchers have concluded that a more appropriate legal drinking age would be 25. This important research finding seems to be confined to technical journals and doesn't usually make it into the mass media. If more parents were exposed to emerging studies on brain development, they might be galvanized to act.

We pointed out earlier some recent state initiatives to lower the drinking age. Given the above, we think that many legislators do not think through the implication of changing this policy; instead they base their rationale on other "factors" seemingly important to them, such as trying to contain and control the problem on school campuses and especially at campus parties. It is unrealistic to expect states to move the drinking age out to 25, but what we are hearing and reading from the scientific community should be sufficient to alarm legislators, school officials, and parents to fight against lowering the current limit, and better still, seek to raise it even higher.

All of this should be sufficiently important to provoke action except for two common human tendencies: first, the tendency to react but not immediately respond to a crisis; and second, the failure to understand the key principles for moving from an immediate response to the kind of change management activities that nourish the new behaviors and create a foundation that enables the changes to last.

For this to happen, many of us will need to change our assumption about what is involved in creating *and sustaining* the outcomes we desire – be they changes in policies, enforcement, or habitual personal and group behavior. What is that flawed paradigm? It is the reasoning that a precipitating event has the power within itself to motivate permanent change; that something that happens in and of itself generally has the teaching and motivational power to sustain that change. Those of us who have worked in the area of change management understand how faulty that premise is. Smart heads of organizations know better than to try and make a lasting change out of a single executive order. See how far that takes them! With a few historic exceptions, the necessary and sufficient forces for creating and sustaining change do not reside in the crises itself but in how we respond to it, both immediately and over time. With only a couple exceptions, very few traumatic events possess the power in and of themselves to do that. This is a function of our thinking that we can do something about!

In the table below are the results of a longitudinal study done on the retention of learning and motivation following the normal "precipitating" factors of change.

How Well Do We Retain the Learning and Motivation to Sustain Change

Precipitating Factor	Retention of Impact, Motivation
Impact Event without Follow Up Goal Planning Support (Example-Plane Crash)	50% within 24 hours 25% within 48 hours 2% within 16 days
Building on Initial Impulse with 6 Space Repetitions around Goals	6X = Up to 62% 15 years to life
Personal Discovery Moment Without Follow-up Goal Planning (Example - Reading book passage)	25% within 24 hours 15% within 48 hours 5% within 16 days
Building on Initial Impulse with 6 Space Repetitions around Goals	6X = Up to 50% 15 years to life

Let's examine the conclusions of this study.

THE NEED FOR IMMEDIATE RESPONSE

We have all experienced insights and/or events which prompted us to shift direction or start down a new path. Most reformed alcoholics will tell you that a particular event or major trigger prompted them to enroll in AA and start the journey towards reform.

Events and breakthrough insights are among the most galvanizing forces in getting our attention, touching our empathies, and bringing us to a point of taking action. The time when we are usually most open to shifting direction or attitude is usually in the face of these experiences, be it a lung x-ray, automobile accident that nearly takes our life, the accidental or intentional death of a child or loved one, failing an importance course credit, etc.

However, as the chart above indicates, the most intense of our feelings about these matters occur within the first 24-48 hours of experiencing them. That seems true of most events and our initial reactions and responses over time to those events. You can probably identify with this common experience: When news story hits about a scandal or a tragedy created by human negligence (or needless deaths caused through youth alcohol consumption), we are stirred. We feel very strongly be it through the expression of anger, sympathy, guilt, etc. We cry out to ourselves or others, "We need to do something about this". But most often we don't, and if we don't do something about it right away, pretty soon the intensity of the emotion subsides and the concerns and interests of daily life begin to replace whatever it was that initially triggered our strong reactions.

Furthermore, not only are we in a better place at that moment to act, but that world whom we must influence is also more vulnerable to the impacts of that event and more open to positively respond to our actions and influences. The lesson here is to respond to what you are convicted or motivated to do within 48 hours of the event.

This is no truer than in our arousal over youth alcohol abuse and prevention. We cringe at the stories or live examples of alcohol's devastation (accident, death, maiming, etc.). It is at the moment having a major effect on us. We are tempted to drop other things and do something about it, but we don't. Over a short period of time, the events have lost their motivational punch and power and other "pressing" concerns take their place. This leads us to the second important conclusion.

THE NECESSARY CONDITION FOR LASTING CHANGE

Whether prompted by a sudden event or cognitive/emotional inspiration, events are strongly impactful enough to make us want to take action. However, these experiences and observations alone, without building additional sustaining support, will not create lasting change. Lasting change, whether through a new policy, changed behavioral norms, new language about alcohol prevention, etc. usually require something more than the precipitating event. We are talking here about the well documented "primacy-recency effect" proven in countless behavioral psychology experiments, and it has probably been personally evident to us throughout our life experiences.

Let me offer a personal example. In one of the neighborhoods where I lived, an older woman widowed for a year was brutally attacked and raped in her home by a young man living in another part of town. We, and our neighbors, were incensed and decided to organize a neighborhood watch to assure that this would never happen again in our community. Most every man in the neighborhood volunteered to serve and was assigned a shift. For the first three months, things worked like clockwork. After that, bereft of no further incidents or getting the watch group together, enthusiasm for serving the assigned "watch" began to abate. Many began to think that since further risk of repetition was small, there was no need to tie up their schedules regularly to be a part of the watch. Within six months, only a few continued to volunteer and holes began to develop in the schedule with no coverage at all during those times, often at night. Eventually the program died. The initial call to action over time lost the power to motivate people.

It is true that certain events have galvanizing effects upon our national psyche and lead to permanent changes. 9/11 is a key example. The traumas experienced were life changing. Most people still remember where they were when these incidents happened and emotions which immediately followed. However, ask yourself, "What drove and sustained the energy to make the security and policy changes we now live under?" It was the ongoing communications and multiple efforts to force security changes supported heavily by government legislation and policy and the press. Many doubt that the strong response to 9/11 would be permanently embedded into our national life and conduct without the active support of the many who worked to put in place more effective strategies to protect us and to prevent this incident from happening again.

As you think about it, not too many events in the past have had that effect? Pearl Harbor? The Kennedy and King assassinations? Vietnam? It was more than the impacts of the event, but what followed, that drove people to make lasting changes in security and civil rights.

One might think that other events, such as the Columbine High School shooting, the Virginia Tech massacre, or the latest Fort Hood mass shootings should have that effect. All three struck a vital arousing nerve. The State and Federal Governments spent billions of dollars in responding to the first two incidents, and the Military will spend money to get at the bottom of the Fort Hood shooting. In the first two cases, a few good changes were made, but the strong immediate post-event impulse to make major changes in on-campus security did not produce measurable change. That led to the inevitable subsiding of the initial pained and angry feelings associated with the needless deaths of young people without substantive action. Memories have been shortened and emotions weakened and fading from our consciousness. Can you name other pivotal events that elicited strong near-term impact and produced massive emotional reactions but with no or tepid efforts to sustain the motivation to change?

Companies that go through major crises have long learned that initial recovery from the incident does not affect the internal changes needed nor change, over time, the perception of those external stakeholders affected by the consequences of the incidents. One of my colleagues, a professional risk and crisis management consultant, has long experienced and studied the "response" curve of organizations in their attempts to recover from a crisis and make their reputation in the community better.

His research demonstrates that companies whose reputation is damaged by an event and who focus only on the immediate response to that incident, not taking the time to work with the affected people over the longer recovery period, end up losing in a couple ways. First, they don't capitalize on the lessons of what to avoid and what to do the next time something occurs; and second, they never recover their reputation to the place where it was before the incident. On the other hand, companies in crisis which take the "recovery" seriously and spend time and resources over the longer haul to help the people through it, not only take home valuable lessons and new applications for the next time, but they more quickly restore their reputation, and in some cases, enhance it. They took the time to learn more fully what they did right and what they did wrong.

The net effect was that everyone became wiser and more diligent about watching for signals of vulnerability and correcting them before they took on more serious consequences. An added benefit normally is a more effective community relationship that encourages their stakeholders to give them the benefit of the doubt should the incident be repeated in the future.

It doesn't take any more print than this to see the applications of these findings to our efforts to change the culture of youth alcohol consumption and abuse. To summarize, **there are six key lessons to be learned about creating effective answers to youth alcohol issues.**

1. Our fullest and most energetic responses to serious or critical incidents, or highly impactful things we read or hear, occur at or very close to the time they happen or are experienced. We are driven by critical incidences, or by information of critical impact that resonates deeply within us. Timing is everything!
2. Done quickly and effectively, these can set in motion the necessary conditions of change provided additional steps are taken.
3. While these incidents are a sufficient condition for action, they are probably not the necessary condition for lasting change. What is normally required is a sustained and energetic effort following them to move their impacts and effects into continuing actions that will sustain the desired changes. The "cause" must be kept in front of people in ways that continue to motivate action. That requires consistent and constant action.
4. The "cause" must be an intelligently serious one, not one based on fleeting emotion. This also includes follow up actions, in order to prevent inertia from setting in. As Andy Grove of Intel wrote, "You can't be a serious innovator of change unless and until you are

ready, willing, and able to seriously play. Serious play is not an oxymoron; it is the essence of innovation and change."

5. That being said, the proven best course of action is for people to respond to what is at first their "temporary" conviction as if it is a real conviction. Even when they see better ways of doing it, the important thing is to start doing it. If there is a better way, the course can be quickly corrected.
6. The surest way to success is to move forward smartly through scheduled goal-driven action and achievement. As one sage said: "If you talk about it, it's a dream. If you start visualizing it, something starts to happen. When you start planning it, it becomes possible. When you schedule it, it becomes real". More about that shortly.

We can be far more successful in the things we do to control and minimize the consequences of youthful drinking. But where do we start? It doesn't have to start off as a full blown strategic plan. It may be a simple beginning, but by all means START doing something about it now.

"Never forget implementation. It's the 'last 98 percent' of the solution to the puzzle."

"You miss 100% of the shots you never take." Wayne Gretzky

Here Are Several Important Ways To Start Becoming An Agent Of Change.

1. Become more self-aware of the transactions you make in your head that drive the way you think about youth and alcohol, the assumptions and rationalizations you may be creating, and the resultant denial and or delay behaviors that result. Examine your values. Are they aligned with your assumptions? What are they telling you to think and do? Make sure to delve into what is deeply real to you, not only what you habitually verbalized. The power of our assumptions is explained at the end of the chapter.

   "You must be the change you wish to see in the world." Gandhi

2. Spend some time learning and assimilating the proven principles of interventional change and influence. Given the particular situation of the motivating incident or reading that aroused you, what is the best way to enable it to be transformed into change? Change management principles are simple to memorize but often harder to put into practice. However, when implemented, it makes the work of influence and advocacy much more effective. And as an added bonus, these time-tested principles are good for other life situations - business, family, or personal development. Some change tips are located at the end of the chapter.

3. Learn how experienced prevention and intervention professionals addressed similar situations. The literature and case studies on personal intervention are numerous. We mention a couple good resources at the end of the chapter. Most of us have been in close family situations where we have had to confront our desire to intervene when kids, siblings, cousins, or in laws are in conflict that they cannot resolve and seem to need a third party to help them

through it. If we can learn to intervene in smart and timely ways, the results can be well worth the pain of their initial reactions to us. In many instances, an intervention is just what is needed before things get out of control and further damage or violence ensues. As a side note in this regard, experts tell us that an intervention by an entire intact family can have more impact that one by a single individual.

4. Remember that whatever course we take to change things, timing is usually everything. Strike while the fire is hot or it's often too late. I remember a time, as an administrator in a large city school system, when several students got into a fight at a Friday night event. It was broken up by several who were not involved, including local police, but it was clear that the hostility had not abated, and I had not been told about it and the perpetrators. When school opened on Monday, one of the students involved on Friday night brought a weapon in and killed another student with whom he had fought.

   I sought out the witnesses and law enforcement partners from the Friday night incident and said to them, "If you would have called, I would have immediately gone to the individual's homes and done an intervention." From that unfortunate experience, we learned to deputize individuals to either intervene on the spot or quickly communicate what is happening to those who can intervene. That was a real lesson learned. My staff and I began to take seriously the critical element of timing and purposed to intervene in disputes and incidents quickly.

5. Understand how to optimize systems to make and sustain changes. Individual efforts to intervene and make a difference are great, as far as they go. However, alcohol abuse generally is a systemic problem and generates more widespread consequences than a single individual, no matter how charismatic, can effect through single interventions. We need committed groups and leaders who can arouse and organize others into a "cause" mentality. This is why it is always important to have a community-based coalition in place to respond to critical incidences or events that require long-term policy and program action.

A key system to understand and work with is the political process. It represents a more promising area of accomplishment, yet most shy away from it, insecure about political activism and the ponderous process they fear might be involved. We need people who will commit to taking on advocacy around alcohol related legislation that could make a real difference. True, it is not easy, takes patience, and one can expect ferocious opposition, but the voice of enough "everyday people" does get heard. Targets that have already had a sympathetic hearing but where the needle has yet to be significantly moved is in pushing for higher taxes on alcohol, limiting the expansion of new alcohol sales outlets, and limiting the hours in which these beverages can be sold.

One of the "tricks" is to make it hard for a key legislator to miss an important underage drinking caucus or meeting. There are ways to respectfully put on the pressure to attend - by infusing the event with other "power sources" of influence (media, community action groups, etc.) that can use used to "close the deal". If you are interested but deterred by the effort it would take you to create and garner the necessary mass of advocates to be heard, there are other already established groups in which you can participate and be an influencer. Be active in groups like MADD, Drug-Free Community Coalitions or school-based prevention efforts. These groups can help drive the long-term political change necessary to affect change.

6. Be constantly open to where new possibilities and avenues might exist for multiplying your initial efforts. In my hometown of Alexandria, Virginia a developer proposed eliminating a wooded area enjoyed by our community and wanted to replace it with mini-mansions. I was stunned by how many people showed up at a town meeting several of us organized. Because I live in the Washington, DC area, many of my neighbors are lawyers and advocates. Within an hour, we developed a strategy to prevent and stop the action of the developer. I was impressed how this collection of lawyers and advocates could turn their skills into a formidable action that achieved our goal. Later that evening, however, I was to be challenged by a

young mom who was no lawyer, no advocate but a concerned parent.

Lisa knocked on our door about 7:30 PM. She introduced herself and said she lived in the cul-de-sac near our home. I will never forget her first words. "I understand that you and your wife are community organizers." I proudly affirmed her suspicion. She then said, "I need your help." She went on to explain to me that the main street that leads out of our neighborhood and accesses the local elementary school is heavily trafficked and is very dangerous for her children and others to cross. "We need a cross walk with blinking lights," she asserted. She went on to say that she couldn't get anybody to listen to her at the school, at the county, or at the state. "I am being given more bureaucratic nonsense as to why my request is impossible", she said. Impossible always gets my attention.

We invited Lisa in and, over a long cup of coffee, asked her a hundred questions. She had answers to most of them but clearly needed some help navigating through the bureaucracy. We discovered in talking with her that five years earlier a child and her grandfather had been killed crossing the street while heading to the playground on the school campus. She kept saying, "Someday another child is going to get killed crossing that street, and I don't want it to be one of mine." My wife and I took on the challenge. We would help Lisa get her cross walk. I explained that given our travel and other responsibilities, she would have to do most of the foot work, as time was a premium. She agreed.

Over the course of the next 14 months we met with county supervisors, state delegates to the Commonwealth of Virginia, and local and state law enforcement. We had support but no action. The excuses never stopped. We learned more about the protocols and procedures for putting in a crosswalk than we ever dreamed. There were days when we were all sorely tempted to sneak out and paint the crosswalk ourselves. Eventually, the neighborhood, hearing of our roadblocks and barriers, mobilized and the lawyers and advocates went back to work. I will never forget the feeling I had when I came home from work one evening and saw the crosswalk complete with blinking yellow lights and signs.

Lisa did it. She never gave up, and she process taught volumes about creating or making change within a bureaucracy. What started out as an effort to stop a developer from building mini-mansions was now a cause to place crosswalks at intersections where children crossed. Before it was over, Lisa was responsible for putting in over six different crosswalks that were approaches to the school.

Though not directly related to the theme of this book, this illustration shows how success can be yours when someone (perhaps you?) creates a focused starting point and arouses a community to take action against what seem to be insurmountable resistance and problems. Who knows? You could be the answer your community is looking for...

EXAMPLES OF THOSE WHO DECIDED TO MAKE A DIFFERENCE

Stories abound in our history about how aroused talented, motivated individuals and groups of people make a difference. My thoughts often turn to the United Airlines Flight

93 tragedy and what aroused leadership did to save possibly thousands of lives without worrying unduly about what was going to happen to them.

The leadership that formed as the crisis was unfolding deserves a case study award. When it became evident that the normal expected itinerary of that flight had became a tool in the hands of terrorists and the plane was headed to Washington, DC to do major and possibly fatal damage to the heart of our government, take note of what a group of self-appointed, brave, and committed leaders did to save a far larger disaster from happening. Their actions followed the following principles of great leadership:

1. They quickly gathered the information as to what was going on using cell phones to talk to family members on the ground and sizing up the logistics and context of the cabins, what to do, and who to target.
2. They assessed their current skills. Among them were a former cop, jujitsu instructor

and pilot. They asked "what do we have here that we can use?"

3. They weighed their options, a very fundamental step.
4. They made a collective decision through "voting" - very important to get total ownership. The fact that these passengers took the time to vote is evidence that they knew these actions needed to be a group decision.
5. They executed with abandonment - regardless of the outcome.

This is an excellent model of group leadership taking the right steps to address this extremely significant problem - one of life and death. We are in such a struggle to save our youth, and likewise need a similar model of leadership to take on the very serious problem of youth alcohol consumption and abuse. Think about it. We have plenty of information available to help us size up the problem and the attitudinal and political context in which it is festering. There are many tools to help us and our group to determine where to focus their capabilities to address the problems. We have already laid out several proven options for action. What is now needed is the collective decision of a committed group to seize these resources and make a difference.

Project Freedom

Here is one instance when these principles of leadership were put into practices and aroused leaders effected a needed change. While I was an educator in the Wichita, Kansas school system, for several weeks the city had been bedeviled by gang violence. In fact, eleven had been either killed or critically maimed in the period of a month. Several of us, greatly concerned about the increasing pattern of violence, *immediately assessed the situation* (Principle 1); decided *to target young gang members* (Principle 1); *used our experiences and skills* to create an organization called Project Freedom, consisting of leaders from prevention, education, law enforcement, treatment and continuing care. Soon, business, faith leaders, political leaders, and corporate executives joined the cause. In the course of three years, over 23,000 people participated in Project Freedom events and the Kansas Health Foundation made a $2 million commitment to support programs and evaluation (Principle 2); *weighed the options* that would make the most difference by doing an extensive needs assessment and asset assessment to determine our capacity to drive change (Principle 3); *decided on a plan* that involved community task forces and work groups to shape a direction that they could embrace (Principle 4); utilized the media to tell our story and to create a system of accountability (Principle 5). At first the media was skeptical until we were able to present them with measurable goals and demonstrated outcomes. Soon, a cartoon was published showing Wichita as a Sleeping Giant being strapped down by gang members. But in the hands of the sleeping giant were a pair of scissors with a label of Project Freedom, the name of our coalition. This re-positioned our work before the community in a significant way and helped to generate significant private sector resources. The response was amazing with thousands of people agreeing to cooperate with, and participate in, the activities laid out by Project Freedom.

That effort provided a wonderful short-term boost in the elimination of gang violence, but on its own, would not have been sustaining. What we further needed was a sustained effort to keep this at the top of people's minds. Over the next three years, we did street interventions, provided scholarships to better engage potential gang members in the educational system, set up an Underground Railroad to help relocate kids in gangs that were being threatened by older gang members, created a jobs program funded by local business for over 500 young people, set up teen pregnancy resource centers in each of the high schools to keep young mothers in school, facilitated graffiti removal programs and brokered mentoring and tutoring programs in each of the high risk neighborhoods. These are only a few of the initiatives that captured the attention of Project Freedom. On the underage drinking front, Project Freedom coordinated sting operations on bad retailers selling to minors, rewarded good retailers for obeying the law, and generated MOUs with all retailers on opening and closing hours. Project Freedom generated measurable results that captured national attention from Time Magazine and 20/20. Time Magazine, after comparing Project Freedom's work with other communities throughout the nation, said, "At least Project Freedom saves lives."[60]

Safe Streets

At the same time that Project Freedom was launching its initiative in Wichita, the City of Tacoma in Pierce County, Washington was launching *Safe Streets*. Safe Streets is the longest continuing Substance Abuse and Violence Prevention Coalition in the history of this country. Responding to high numbers in ten substance abuse and youth violence, citizens came together and brokered partnerships with government, business, and the faith community to take back their streets and make them safe for all of its citizens. They knew that they were not going to be able to arrest their way out of the problem. Safe Streets leadership focused on prevention and intervention strategies that were anchored in strategic planning and targeted goals. Planning, building on systems of inclusivity, transparency in execution, and brokering private/public partnerships, Safe Streets changed the way people did business in Pierce County. Today, they are a statewide force shaping prevention, law enforcement, and treatment strategies throughout the State.

Project Freedom and Safe Streets were not created in University Laboratories or in the midst of abstract think tanks. They were born out of the real life experiences of community leaders responding to a crisis. I have learned much from my wife, Colleen Copple, the former Colleen Minson from Salt Lake City, a strong Mormon mom living in a neighborhood that had experienced over 200 drive-by shootings in one year. Incensed that her six children were caught in the crossfire of a gang shoot-out (fortunately no one was hurt), she decided to engage, and engage she did. She organized other mothers in an effort to stop the violence. They opened their arms to high risk youth; they created activities and events to engage families affected by Gang Violence; and they worked with local law enforcement and the Mayor's office to launch programs and initiatives that would change their city. She needed resources, so she wrote a grant to the State Juvenile Justice Department and was awarded a $40,000 grant to fund prevention activities. This was her first grant, but it was only the beginning. Four years later, when she left Salt Lake City to move to Washington, DC, the Salt Lake Tribune referred to her as the $10 Million Woman. Attorney General Janet Reno and Senator Orin Hatch each presented her awards for outstanding leadership in the comprehensive communities' initiative. She took on gangs, substance abuse, Methamphetamine labs, and drug endangered children. She did planning for law enforcement, prevention, and the Mayor's office. This is an individual who took a crisis and turned it into a strategy.

Things You Can Do

1. Reach out to substance abuse prevention organizations in your community and state and ask what they are doing to monitor the price of alcohol in your state. Many studies have found that higher alcohol prices lead to lower consumption and fewer alcohol-related problems.
2. Find out how licenses to serve alcohol are regulated in your community. Make sure that you know when a new alcohol license is being considered. Learn about alcohol outlet violations in your community, particularly service to minors. Pay attention to where outlets are located (near schools, playgrounds, etc.) and the ordinances that may limit the number of outlets.
3. Advocate for enhanced enforcement of minimum 21 drinking age laws, particularly in establishments in your community that have a history of selling to minors.
4. Monitor the drink promotions and advertising around college or university campuses. Pay attention to how these establishments promote their products to college-age drinkers.

5. Include problem drinking establishments as part of neighborhood or business watch programs. Work with law enforcement to help monitor problem drinking establishment behaviors.

GETTING AT YOUR WORKING ASSUMPTIONS

When someone is asked how he or she would behave under certain circumstances, the answer usually given is that person's *espoused theory* of action for that situation. This is the theory of action to which he or she gives allegiance and communicates to others. However, the theory that actually governs one's actions is what is called *theory-in-use*. Making this distinction allows us to ask questions about the extent to which our behavior fits espoused theory; and whether inner feelings become truly being expressed in actions. In other words, is there congruence between the two? Effective living results from developing congruence between theory-in-use and espoused theory. For example, in explaining our actions to a colleague we may call upon some convenient piece of theory, such as "I want to be a part of alcohol prevention efforts" and explain to others our concerns, or even to ourselves at some level. The theory-in-use might be quite different. We may want to "sound good", but don't put our feet to any efforts to address the problems. A key role of reflection, we could argue, is to reveal the theory-in-use and to explore the nature of the 'fit', not only in relationship to the subject of this book, but everything in our life we "espouse." [61]

Tips on Effectively Managing Change (To Increase the Probabilities for Success)

- Check and modify your own attitudes first. Ask "If the situation is changing, in what ways do I need to change?"
- Total honesty with self and others gets you further than avoidance or surprises.
- There is no such thing as over-communication or over-education.
- Protect core values at all costs during the change (quality, service, integrity, etc.)
- Don't lose sight of overarching priorities, vision, values, and mission. Keep them constantly before you as the "North Star".
- Carefully select some change sponsors who will support and effectively encourage you during a period of change. Identify and attend to their key concerns before starting.

The right people for this may not be the popular choices.

- Establish short term "hard" goals and benchmarks as rein forcers. Use quick wins to build confidence in yourself and trust and loyalty in others.
- Move as fast as you can. Remember that the old has the edge until people learn how to do things differently.
- Over-communicate what is expected to yourself and others. Find new channels and ways to reinforce the needed messages.
- Always push resistance out into the open, whether within yourself or others.
- Be honest and minimize surprises as much as possible.
- Monitor frequently. Ride herd. Look for bad news. Don't be afraid to change in the midst of change.
- Continually analyze vulnerabilities. Get trusted eyes and ears, outside and inside, to help. Most of us have a functional blindness to our vulnerabilities, personal and organizational.
- Analyze your internal systems for anything that doesn't support the priorities of the change, (i.e. processes, training, products/services, organizational climate, etc.)
- Pay attention to the structures (in your mind and in the outside world). Structures are like the walls and corridors of a building that control the flow of human energy. Ask, "Are

these controls working right? Focusing the energy right?"

- Change norms about "How I, or we, are really doing around these matters (with the changes). Unattended, old norms usually trump new change efforts.
- Know your key communication "controllers and distributors" even if they are not a formal part of the structure. You really need their help to get to some people who are not accessed by normal channels.
- Pay attention to leadership styles adjusting to the particular level of readiness in each person you are influencing.
- Adopt reinforcement and reward practices to support the change priorities. Raise the bar, motivate, and then reward.
- Give psychological paychecks: encouragement, compliments, etc.

CONCLUSION

Hanging on the wall of my office is a plaque presented to me by Project Freedom when I left Wichita and moved to Washington, DC. Its message has resonated with me over many years. *A task without a vision is drudgery; a vision without a task is a dream; a vision with a task is the hope of the world.* That is so true in our efforts to build and develop a drug-free community. Preventing alcohol use among underage drinkers will require vision; it will require tasks that are anchored in a strategic plan; and it will require resolve to develop persistent and consistent messages.

Communities will join your efforts as you clearly articulate a plan, propose a strategy, and challenge funders to become partners in your efforts. The Fatal Attraction can be addressed and the warnings about its harms and dangers can be understood as we develop messages that are consistent and resonate with our nation's young people. We have attached a list of organizational resources that will provide additional information and channel your efforts towards effective research and evaluation. Innovate, implement, evaluate, and replicate programs, policies, and strategies that will prevent youth involvement with alcohol. Your actions in the end, while difficult to measure, will save lives.

EXAMPLES OF INTERVENTIONS

The following programs incorporate the NIAAA recommended strategies for effective early intervention: cognitive-behavioral skills enhancement combined with norms clarification and motivational enhancement, personalized feedback regarding alcohol use and associated risk, and challenging alcohol expectancies. Utilizing a harm-reduction approach, these early interventions aim to motivate students to decrease alcohol-related risk and harm. You can access them at www.campushealthandsafety.org/effectiveprevention/eit/earlyintervention/examples/. While certain elements of these programs may be completed as take-home activities or online, the following interventions are generally delivered face-to-face by a trained practitioner.

Alcohol Skills Training Program (ASTP) was created by the Addictive Behaviors Research Center at the University of Washington. The ASTP was originally presented in eight, 90-minute sessions, but the schedule is flexible and can be adjusted to suit a particular site. During the ASTP practitioners facilitate group discussions around alcohol abuse and dependence issues, providing accurate information about the consequences of alcohol use. Practitioners use motivational enhancement to diminish risky behavior and teach students skills for avoiding alcohol and setting drinking limits. Numerous randomized, controlled trials demonstrate the effectiveness of the program in reducing both the quantity of alcohol consumed per drinking occasion and the typical peak blood alcohol content (BAC) per drinking episode.

Brief Alcohol Screening and Intervention for College Students (BASICS) is a program derived from ASTP and uses a similar blend of strategies. BASICS is a one-on-one intervention conducted in two sessions. The first session consists of a structured clinical interview followed by a student self-report assessment of drinking patterns, attitudes, and alcohol-related consequences. During the second session, the student is presented with the results of their assessment in a non-confrontational manner. Multiple randomized, controlled trials indicate that students who have received BASICS drink less and experience fewer negative consequences when they do choose to drink. These effects remain significant over the months and years following the intervention.

CHOICES was developed using the core principles of ASTP. In this brief group intervention (one or two sessions lasting a total of three hours or less), information about alcohol and related risks is combined with a structured journaling process. In practice, CHOICES has been used as a universal prevention program, as a first response for sanctioned students (indicated prevention), and as a mandatory program for target populations such as fraternities/sororities, athletes, and incoming freshmen (selective prevention). As a variation of ASTP, an evidence-based practice, CHOICES is effective in reducing levels of alcohol consumption and alcohol-related harms.

Web-based Early Interventions. Online and web-based prevention and intervention programming can be useful for serving a larger segment of the at-risk population. As part of a comprehensive approach, and incorporating NIAAA recommended strategies, these interventions can effectively reduce heavy drinking and related consequences without face to face interaction.

www.Alcohol.Edu is an interactive assessment and personalized feedback tool for college students. This three-hour online program also provides information on the social, physical, and biological effects of alcohol use. www.Alcohol.Edu offers specialized curricula focusing on the general college population and sanctioned students with an additional course presented in a brief motivational interviewing style available to purchasers of AlcoholEdu. Limited evidence suggests that AlcoholEdu may produce slight changes in attitude and behavior.

Check Up To Go (CHUG) (http://www.echeckuptogo.com/usa/) is a brief drinking behavior assessment and feedback tool. A student can take the CHUG in a paper-and-pencil format or online (e-CHUG). The CHUG/e-CHUG method of feedback delivery employs motivational interviewing in concert with personalized feedback derived from the assessment to encourage a student to reduce his or her alcohol consumption and related risk. In one randomized controlled study, e-CHUG significantly reduced the average drink consumption per week in male college students.

www.myStudentBody.com is an interactive website containing modules specific to alcohol, other drugs, tobacco, STDs, stress, and nutrition. The alcohol portion utilizes a BASICS-derived risk-assessment tool called Rate Myself. Using the results of this assessment, immediate personalized feedback on the student's alcohol use, beliefs, and consequences is presented in graphic form. myStudentBody.com also provides information to students about a variety of alcohol-related issues such as drug interactions, financial impacts, and state alcohol laws and policies. In a randomized controlled clinical trial, www.myStudentBody.com participants reported decreases in heavy episodic drinking and fewer negative consequences related to alcohol. These effects were sustained through a three month follow up.[62]

SBIRT - Screening, Brief Intervention, and Referral to Treatment is a strategy that encourages and promotes brief interventions by medical doctors and others at the time of a medical exam. However, the strategy can be used by teachers, employers, and others if they suspect alcohol use in an underage drinker. By asking a simple question about alcohol use, it suggests an intervention that can lead to possible referrals for either treatment or counseling. You can gather other details on SBIRT from SAMHSA or the Office of Drug Control Policy.

Organizations with a Connection to Alcohol Issues

Name/Website	Contact Information
ORGANIZATIONS	
U.S. Department of the Treasury Alcohol and Tobacco Tax and Trade Bureau	Public Information Officer 1310 G Street, NW., Suite 300 Washington, D.C. 20220; www.ttb.gov 202-453-2000
American Academy of Pediatrics (AAP)	141 Northwest Point Boulevard Elk Grove Village, IL 60007-1098 847-434-4000 or 601 13th Street, NW Suite 400 North Washington, DC 20005 202-347-8600 www.aap.org
American Beverage Licensees (ABL)	5101 River Road, Suite 108 Bethesda, MD 20816-1560 www.ablusa.org 301-656-1494
American College of Mental Health Administration (ACMHA)	7804 Loma del Norte Road NE Albuquerque, NM 87109-5419 www.acmha.org 505-822-5038
American Society of Addiction Medicine (ASAM)	4601 N. Park Avenue, Upper Arcade #101 Chevy Chase, MD 20815 www.asam.org 301-656-3920
The Beer Institute	122 C Street NW, Suite 350 Washington, DC 20001 www.beerinstitute.org 202-737-2337

Community Anti-Drug Coalitions of America (CADCA)	625 Slaters Lane Suite 300 Alexandria, VA 22314 www.cadca.org 1-800-54-CADCA
Center for Science in the Public Interest (CSPI)	1875 Connecticut Avenue, NW Suite 300 Washington, DC 20009 www.cspinet.org 202-332-9110
The Century Council (TCC)	2345 Crystal Drive Suite 910 Arlington, VA 22202 www.centurycouncil.org 202-637-0077
The Distilled Spirits Council	1250 Eye Street, NW, Suite 400 Washington, D.C. 20005 www.discus.org 202-628-3544
Ensuring Solutions to Alcohol Problems	2021 K Street NW Suite 800 Washington, DC 20006 www.ensuringsolutions.org 202-994-4303
Faces and Voices of Recovery	1010 Vermont Ave. #708 Washington, DC 20005 www.facesandvoicesofrecovery.org 202-737-0690
International Association of Chiefs of Police	515 North Washington St Alexandria, VA, 22314 www.theiacp.org 703-836-6767
Leadership to Keep Children Alcohol Free Foundation	2933 Lower Bellbrook Rd. Spring Valley, OH 45370-9001 www.alcoholfreechildren.org 937-848-2993
Legal Action Center (LAC)	225 Varick Street New York, NY 10014 212-243-1313 236 Massachusetts Ave. NE Suite 505 Washington, D.C. 20002-4980 202-544-5478 www.lac.org
Lions Clubs International	300 West 22nd Street Oak Brook, IL 60523-8842 www.lionsclubs.org

	630-571-5466
Mothers Against Drunk Driving (MADD)	511 E. John Carpenter Freeway Suite 700 Irving, TX 75062 www.madd.org 214-744-6233
The National Alcohol Beverage Control Association (NABCA)	4401 Ford Avenue, Suite 700 Alexandria, VA 22302-1473 www.nabca.org 703-578-4200
National Alliance for Model State Drug Laws (NAMSD)	1414 Prince Street, Suite 312 Alexandria, VA 22314 www.namsdl.org 703-836-6100
National Association of Addiction Treatment Providers (NAATP)	313 W. Liberty Street, Suite 129, Lancaster, PA 17603-2748 www.naatp.org 717-392-8480
National Association of Counties	25 Massachusetts Avenue, NW Washington, DC 20001 www.naco.org 202-393-6226
National Association for Children of Alcoholics (NACOA)	11426 Rockville Pike, Suite 301 Rockville, Maryland 20852 www.nacoa.net 301-468-0985
National Association of Drug Court Professionals (NADCP)	4900 Seminary Road, Suite 320, Alexandria, Virginia 22310 www.nadcp.org 703-575-9400
National Association of School Nurses	8484 Georgia Avenue, Suite 420, Silver Spring, MD 20910 www.nasn.org 240-821-1130
National Association of State Alcohol and Drug Abuse Directors (NASADAD)	1025 Connecticut Avenue NW, Suite 605, Washington, DC 20036 www.nasadad.org 202-293-0090

National Center on Addiction and Substance Abuse at Columbia University (CASA)	633 Third Avenue, 19th Floor New York, NY 10017-6706 www.casacolumbia.org 212-841-5200
The National Conference of State Liquor Administrators (NCSLA)	4216 King Street West Alexandria, VA. 22302-1507 www.ncsla.org
National Consumers League (NCL)	1701 K Street, NW, Suite 1200, Washington DC 20006 www.nclnet.org 202-835-3323
National Council on Alcoholism and Drug Dependence(NCADD)	244 East 58th Street 4th Floor New York, NY 10022 www.ncadd.org 212-269-7797
National Liquor Law Enforcement Association (NLLEA)	11720 Beltsville Drive, Suite 900 Calverton, MD 20705 www.nllea.org 301-755-2795
National School Boards Association	1680 Duke Street Alexandria, VA 22314 www.nsba.org 703-838-6722
National Organizations for Youth Safety	7371 Atlas Walk Way #109 Gainesville , VA 20155 www.noys.org 703-981-0264
National Sheriffs Association	1450 Duke St. Alexandria, VA 22314 www.sheriffs.org 703-836-7827
Partnership for a Drug Free America	405 Lexington Avenue, Suite 1601 New York, NY 10174 www.drugfree.org 212-922-1560
Responsible Retailing Forum (RRF)	681 Main Street, Suite 325 Waltham, MA 02451-0621 www.rrforum.org 781-647-0858
State	236 Massachusetts Ave. NE

Associations of Addiction Services (SAAS)	Suite 505 Washington, DC 20002 www.saasnet.org 202-546-4600
Students Against Destructive Decisions (SADD)	255 Main Street Marlborough, MA 01752 www.sadd.org 1-877-SADD-INC
Techniques for Effective Alcohol Management (TEAM)	1800 Diagonal Road, Suite 600 Alexandria, VA 22314 www.teamcoalition.org 703-647-7430
Wine and Spirits Guild of America	3530 Vinings Ridge Court Atlanta, Georgia 30339 www.wineandspiritsguild.com 770-956-8808
Wine and Spirits Wholesalers of America (WSWA)	805 15th St., NW, Suite 430 Washington, DC 20005 www.wswa.org 202-371-9792
World Association of the Alcohol Beverage Industries, Inc. (WAABI)	4211 Oakhill Road Fredericksburg, VA 22408 www.waabi.org 540-891-7202
FEDERAL AGENCIES	
Center for Disease Control and Prevention	1600 Clifton Rd Atlanta, GA 30333 www.cdc.gov 1-800-232-4636
Drug Enforcement Administration (DEA)	Office of Diversion Control 8701 Morrissette Drive Springfield, VA 22152 www.justice.gov/dea/index.htm 202-307-1000
Multijurisdictional	Physical Address

Counterdrug Task Force Training Program (MCTFT)/St. Petersburg College	3200 34th Street South St. Petersburg, FL 33711 Mailing Address P.O. Box 13489 St. Petersburg, FL 33733 www.mctft.com 1-800-243-5550
National Guard	1411 Jefferson Davis Highway Arlington VA 22202-3231 www.ng.mil 1-800-464-8273
National Highway Traffic & Safety Administration	1200 New Jersey Avenue, SE West Building Washington, DC 20590 www.nhtsa.gov 1-888-327-4236
National Institute on Alcoholism and Alcohol Abuse	5635 Fishers Lane, MSC 9304 Bethesda, MD 20892-9304 www.niaaa.nih.gov 301-443-3860
National Institute on Drug Abuse	6001 Executive Boulevard Room 5213 Bethesda, MD 20892-9561 www.nida.nih.gov 301-443-1124
Office of National Drug Control Policy (ONDCP)	P.O. Box 6000 Rockville, MD 20849-6000 www.whitehousedrugpolicy.gov 1-800-666-3332
Substance Abuse and Mental Health Services Administration	1 Choke Cherry Road Rockville, MD 20857 www.samhsa.gov 240-276-2000
SAMHSA's Center for Substance Abuse Prevention	1 Choke Cherry Road Rockville, MD 20857 www.prevention.samhsa.gov
SAMHSA's Center for Substance Abuse Treatment	1 Choke Cherry Road Rockville, MD 20857 www.csat.samhsa.gov
U.S. Department of Education	400 Maryland Avenue, SW Washington, D.C. 20202 www.ed.gov 1-800-USA-LEARN

U.S. Department of Health and Human Services (HHS)	200 Independence Avenue, S.W. Washington, D.C. 20201 www.hhs.gov 1-877-696-6775
U.S. Department of Health and Human Services, Office of Disease Prevention and Health	Tower Building 1101 Wootton Parkway Suite LL100 Rockville, MD 20852 www.odphp.osophs.dhhs.gov 240-453-8280
U.S. Department of Homeland Security, U.S. Immigration and Customs Enforcement	500 12th St, SW Washington, DC 20536 www.ice.gov 1-866-DHS-2-ICE
U.S. Department of Justice, Office of Justice Programs, Community Capacity Development Office	810 Seventh Street, NW Washington, DC 20531 www.ojp.usdoj.gov/ccdo 202-616-1152
U.S. Department of Labor's Working Partners for an Alcohol- and Drug-free Workplace Program	U.S. Department of Labor 200 Constitution Ave., NW Washington, DC 20210 www.dol.gov/workingpartners 1-866-4-USA-DOL
U.S. Department of State, International Narcotics & Law Enforcement (INL)	U.S. Department of State 2201 C Street NW Washington, DC 20520 www.state.gov/p/inl 202-647-4000
Federal Trade Commission - We Don't Serve Teens	600 Pennsylvania Avenue, NW Washington, DC 20580 www.dontserveteens.gov 1-877-FTC-HELP

CORPORATE SUPPORTERS	
Alvarez & Associates	600 Maryland Ave SW Suite 800W Washington, DC 20024 www.alvarezassociates.com 202-580-7422
Consumer Healthcare Products Association	900 19th Street, NW, Suite 700 Washington, DC 20006 www.chpa-info.org 202-429-9260
DirecTV	P.O. Box 6550 Greenwood Village, CO 80155-6550 www.directv.com/DTVAPP/content/corporate/health 1-888-330-7827
Office Depot Foundation	6600 North Military Trail Boca Raton, FL 33496 www.officedepotfoundation.org 706-867-0278
Phamatech	10151 Barnes Canyon Rd. San Diego, CA 92121 www.phamatech.com 858-643-5555
Purdue Pharma	One Stamford Forum 201 Tresser Boulevard Stamford, CT 06901-3431 www.pharma.com 203-588-8000
Reckitt Benckiser	Reckitt Benckiser (North America) Inc. Morris Corporate Center IV 399 Interpace Parkway, P.O. Box 225 Parsippany, NJ 07054-0225 www.rb.com 973-404-2600
King Pharmaceuticals	501 Fifth Street Bristol, Tennessee 37620 www.kingpharm.com 423-989-8000

Pharmaceutical Research and Manufacturers of America (PhRMA)	950 F Street, NW Suite 300 Washington, DC 20004 www.phrma.org 202-835-3400
Treatment Alternatives for Safe Communities (TASC)	1500 N. Halsted Chicago, IL 60642 www.tasc.org 312-787-0208
INTERNATIONAL ORGANIZATIONS	
Department of State, International Narcotics & Law Enforcement (INL)	U.S. Department of State 2201 C Street NW Washington, DC 20520 www.state.gov/p/inl 202-647-4000
United Nations	United Nations Room: GA-57 New York, NY 10017 www.un.org/en 212-963-4475
FEBRAE	Av. Rio Branco 124 / 20º andar - Centro Rio de Janeiro – RJ www.febrae.org.br (21) 2507-8017
Narcotics Affairs Section, U.S. Embassy, Brazil	SES - Av. das Nações, Quadra 801, Lote 03 70403-900 - Brasilia, DF www.brasilia.usembassy.gov (55-61) 3312-7000
Leones Educando	Calle 80 No. 64 - 57 Piso 2 Barranquilla - Colombia www.leones-educando.org/aliados.html (5) 373-2993
MENTOR	Carrera 13 No. 50-78 Piso2 Bogotá – Colombia

	www.mentorcolombia.org 346-6855
Narcotic Affairs Section, U.S. Embassy, Colombia	Carrera 45 No. 24B-27 Bogotá, D.C. Colombia www.bogota.usembassy.gov/nas.html (571) 315-0811
FUNDASALVA	Av. Olímpica y 71 Av. Sur Nº 3718, Col.Escalón Salvador, El Salvador, C.A. www.fundasalva.org.sv (503) 2236-0333
SECCATID	2da. Calle 1-00 Z.10 Ciudad de Guatemala, Guatemala www.seccatid.gob.gt 2-361-2620
Narcotic Affairs Section, U.S. Embassy, Guatemala	1a. avenida 7-59, zona 10 Ciudad de Guatemala, Guatemala www.nasgt.com.gt (502) 2361-1427
USMBHA	211 N. Florence, Suite 101- El Paso, TX 79901 www.borderhealth.org 915-532-1006
CEDRO	Roca y Boloña 271 Miraflores Lima 18 – Perú www.cedro.org.pe (51-1) 447-0748
CRESER	Calle José Nicolás Rodrigo Nº 580, Urb. Los Pinos - Surco Lima 33 – Perú www.crecer.gob.pe (51-1) 345-2323
IES	Calle Republica de Chile 641 Lima - Perú www.ies.org.pe/Aliados_MR.htm 511-1-433-6314
PRIZMA	Oficina Central: Calle Carlos Gonzáles N°251 Urbanización Maranga Lima 32 - Perú www.prisma.org.pe (51-1) 616-5500
SUMBI	Jr. Juan Pazos 105 - Alt. Cdra.

	3 de la Av. Bolognesi Barranco - Lima, Peru www.sumbi.org.pe (51-1) 247-3067
Narcotic Affairs Section, U.S. Embassy, Peru	Avenida La Encalada cdra. 17 s/n Surco, Lima 33, Peru www.lima.usembassy.gov/public_affairs_section.html (51-1) 618-2000
SANCA	5 Ryder Road Bordeaux, Randburg 2194 www.sancanational.org.za 27 11 781-6410
TASC	1616 North Fort Myer Drive 11th Floor Arlington, VA 22209 www.tascteam.com/southafrica.html (703) 528-7474

ABOUT THE AUTHOR

James E. Copple is the President of the International Institute for Alcohol Awareness, Founding Principal Partner for Strategic Applications International, and Senior Policy Analyst for the Pacific Institute for Research and Evaluation. He was the founding President of Community Anti-Drug Coalitions of America and the former Executive Vice President and Chief Operating Officer of the National Crime Prevention Council. Copple has 20 years experience working in the substance abuse prevention, treatment, and enforcement field. A former college professor, school administrator, and teacher, Copple is a highly regarded public speaker and writer on substance abuse and youth violence. Currently, he and his wife Colleen are working in Africa on mobilizing communities to respond to the HIV/AIDS pandemic in Swaziland and Kenya. A self described "do-gooder" driven by a passion to implement informed and science-based strategies to end poverty, disease, and addiction, Copple believes in the power of communities to guide and direct their own transformation and change. Copple lives in a blended family with 8 children and 15 grandchildren.

END NOTES

[1] *Ninth Special Report to the U.S. Congress on Alcohol and Health from the Secretary of Health and Human Services.* Rockville, MD: USDHHS, Public Health Service, Alcohol, Drug Abuse and Mental Health Administration, National Institute of Alcohol Abuse and Alcoholism, June 1997. Kann, L., Warren, C., et al., Youth risk Behavior Surveillance – Unites States, 1995. *Morb Mortal Wkly Rep CDC Surveillance Summaries*, 45(4):1-84, September 27, 1996.
[2] Reducing Underage Drinking: A Collective Responsibility
[3] Youth Risk Surveillance – United States, 1999. June 9, 2000 / 49(SS05);1-96. L. Kann, S. Kinchen, B. Williams, J. Ross, R. Lowry, J. Grunbaum, and L. Kolbehttp://www.cdc.gov/mmwr/preview/mmwrhtml/ss4905a1.htm, accessed June 19, 2001.
[4] Reducing Underage Drinking: A Collective Responsibility.
[5] Calculated using the 2003 National Survey on Drug Use and Health. J. Gfroerer of the Substance Abuse and Mental Health Services Administration, e-mail to David H. Jernigan, Ph.D., September 14, 2004.
[6] Ellickson, P., Tucker, J., and Klein, D. Ten-year prospective study of public health problems associated with early drinking. *Pediatrics* 111(5):949-955, 2003.
[7] Grant, B., and Dawson, D. Age at onset of alcohol use and its association with DSM-IV alcohol abuse and dependence: Results from the National Longitudinal Alcohol Epidemiologic Survey. *Journal of Substance Abuse,* Vol. 9, Jan. 1998. pp. 103-110.
[8] This section about Jeff and his son was written from documents provided by Jeff and as told by Jeff in 2005 when he was a spokesperson for the International Institute for Alcohol Awareness.
[9] (http://www-fars.nhtsa.dot.gov/Main/index.aspx)
[10] (NHTSA, Traffic Safety Facts, 2007 Data, DOT HS 810 993).
[11] (10th Special Report to Congress on Alcohol and Health, Forward by Donna Shalala)
[12]Reducing Underage Drinking: A Collective Responsibility.
[13] Miller, T.R., Levy, D.T., Spicer, R.S, & Taylor, D.M. (2006). Societal costs of underage drinking, Journal of Studies on Alcohol, 67(4), 519-528, accessed on 11/23/09 at **http://www.udetc.org/UnderageDrinkingCosts.asp.**
[14] Ibid.

[15] Levy, D.T., Miller, T.R., & Cox, K.C. (2003). Underage drinking: societal costs and seller profits. Working Paper. Calverton, MD: PIRE.
[16] T. S.Dee,"The Effects of Minimum Legal Drinking Ages on Teen Childbearing," *Journal of Human Resources* 36, no. 4 (Fall 2001): 824
[17] R.W. Hingson et al.,"Magnitude of Alcohol-Related Mortality and Morbidity among U.S. College Students Ages 18-24," *Journal of Studies on Alcohol* 63 (March 2002): 136-44.
[18] Ibid.
[19] J McGinnis & W Foege, "Actual Causes of Death in the United States," Journal of the American Medical Association {JAMA}, Vol. 270, No. 18, 11/10/93, p. 2208
[20] Levy, D.T., Miller, T.R., & Cox, K.C. (2003). Underage drinking: societal costs and seller profits. Working Paper. Calverton, MD: PIRE.
[21] CASA White Paper. (May 2006). The Commercial Value of Underage and Pathological Drinking to the Alcohol Industry. New York, NY: The National Center on Addiction and Substance Abuse at Columbia University.
[22] Anheuser-Busch InBev Annual Report 2008, accessed on 11/24/09 at http://www.anheuser-busch.com/AnnualReports.html.
[23] Currency Conversion is based on the 2008 yearly average 1 U.S. dollar to 0.683 Euros found at http://france.usembassy.gov/irs-euro.html.
[24] A significant percentage of the total alcohol consumption in the United States each year is by underage youth. The U.S. Substance Abuse and Mental Health Services Administration reports that the percentage is over 11 percent.Household Survey, 2004, Substance Abuse Mental Health Administration, U.S. Department of Health and Human Services.
[25] *Advertising Age*, Jul 19, 2004, p.S-3
[26] Molson Coors Brewing Company Annual Report 2008, accessed on 11/24/09 at http://phx.corporate-ir.net/phoenix.zhtml?c=101929&p=irol.reportsannual.
[27] Diageo Summary Review 2009, accessed on 11/24/09 at http://www.diageo.com/enrow/investors/financialreports/2009/financialreports2009.
[28] Currency Conversion is based on the June 2008 exchange rate of 1 U.S. dollar to 0.509 British pounds sterling found at http://www.x-rates.com/cgi-bin/hlookup.cgi.
[29] SABMiller plc Annual Report 2009, accessed on 11/24/09 at http://sabmiller.com/index.asp?oageid=85.
[30] Study Published January 2006 edition of the Journal of American Public Health. Authored by Kypros Kypri, Robert B. Voas, John D. Langley, Shawn C.R. Stephenson, Dorothy J. Begg, A. Scott Tippetts, and Gabrielle S. Davie.

[31] Office of Juvenile Justice and Delinquency Prevention. *Drinking in America: Myths, Realities, and Prevention Policy*. Washington, DC: U.S. Department of Justice, Office of Justice Programs, Office of Juvenile Justice and Delinquency Prevention, 2005. Available at http://www.udetc.org/documents/Drinking_in_America.pdf* (PDF).
[32] The Impact of Underage Drinking Laws on Alcohol-Related Fatal Crashes of Young Drivers. *Alcoholism: Clinical & Experimental Research*, July 2009.
[33] Harold D. Holder, *Alcohol and the Community: A Systems Approach to Prevention*, (International Research Monographs in the Addictions, Cambridge: Cambridge University Press, 1998) 74.
[34] Holder, -75.
[35] Beer Pong is a popular underage drinking game that is played at parties and in some drinking establishments. It is about getting "smashed" the fastest.
[36] *Drinking in America: Myths, Realities, and Prevention Policy*: U.S. Department of Justice, Office of Juvenile Justice and Delinquency Prevention, 1999.
[37] Substance Abuse and Mental Health Services Administration. (2009). *Results from the 2008 National Survey on Drug Use and Health: National Findings:* 31. (Office of Applied Studies, NSDUH Series H-36, HHS Publication No. SMA 09-4434). Rockville, MD.
[38]*Drinking in America*: 1
[39]*Drinking in America*: 2
[40]Luke 9:46-48, *The New Oxford Annotated Bible*, Edited by Herbert G. May and Bruce M. Metzger, (Oxford University Press: New York), 1973.
[41] Core Competencies for Clergy and Other Pastoral Ministers in Addressing Alcohol and Drug Dependence and the Impact on Family Members, *Substance Abuse and the Family: Defining the Role of the Faith Community*, a Report of an Expert Consensus Panel Meeting, February 26-27, 2003. (Washington, DC).
[42] 2009 WORLD Magazine, October 04, 2008, Vol. 23, No. 20.
[43] Families and Schools Together (F.A.S.T) operates in Wisconsin schools and targets the families of potential drop-outs. It provides eight-week sessions hosted by educators and community volunteers who attempt to build bonds of trust between the families, community, and schools and create supportive networks that children can use as their education progresses. The program also has components to address substance-abuse problems.
[44] Good Shepherd Services in New York, NY is a faith-based program that has involved the community with at-risk youth for almost 150 years. Community members provide tutoring and mentor relationships for

students in local high schools. The program also provides job training and support services for family members of at-risk students who are often, themselves, at need for community support.

[45] Harold Holder, *Alcohol and the Community: A Systems Approach to Prevention*, (Cambridge University Press: Cambridge) 1998. .

[46] Press Release, *New Survey Reveals Alarming Data on Moms, Daughters and Underage Drinking*, The Century Council, December 12, 2005.

[47] IBID

[48] IBID

[49] *National Survey of American Attitudes on Substance Abuse X: Teens and Parents*, conducted by QEV Analytics for the National Center on Addiction and Substance Abuse at Columbia University, August 2005, 2.

[50] National *Survey of American Attitudes on Substance Abuse X: Teens and Parents*, 25.

[51] Karol L. Kumpfer and Rose Alvarado, *Family-Strengthening Approaches for the Prevention of Youth Problem Behaviors*, American Psychologist, Vol. 58, No 6/7, June/July 2003 p. 457.

[52] Kumpfer and Alvarado, *Family-Strengthening*, p. 457.

[53] Kumpfer and Alvarado, *Family-Strengthening*, p. 457.

[54] Issue Brief, *Youth Helping America: The Role of Social Institutions in Teen Volunteering*, Corporation for National & Community Service, 1201 New York Ave., NW, Washington DC, November 2005.

[55] IBID

[56] Tremper, Charles, and Mosher, James. Assessing State Readiness to Act on Alcohol Tax Research Findings, Pacific Institute for Research and Evaluation.

[57] Drinking in America: Myths, Realities, and Prevention Policy. The Underage Drinking Enforcement Training Center. August 2002, funded by the Office of Juvenile Justice and Delinquency, U.S. Department of Justice.

[58] http://web.mlsnet.com/news, July 13, 2009.

[59] National Institutes of Health. *Binge Drinking Puts the Brain, and Life Itself, at Risk*, Nov 7, HealthDay News.

[60] Time Magazine, August 22, 1992.

[61] Argyris, C., & Schön, D. (1978) *Organizational learning: A theory of action perspective*, Reading, Mass: Addison Wesley

[62] United States Department of Education, Higher Education Center for Alcohol Abuse Prevention, 2007.

Disclaimer:
Because involvement with the Alcohol Industry is so controversial, I want to inform the readers that the International Institute for Alcohol Awareness has received funds from the Spirits industry to promote prevention and intervention activities on the college campus and to conduct research around policy areas. At no time have they influenced our outcomes any more than a government agency, when we have been funded, might have influenced our outcomes.

Interviews and events found in this book have taken place over the course of 20 years. If I have misstated any event or mischaracterized any activity, it is my responsibility and mine alone. I depended on journals and my memory of events - I have discovered that the older I get, the less confident I am in my memory. However, I believe that I got it right at least 99% of the time.

www.ingramcontent.com/pod-product-compliance
Ingram Content Group UK Ltd.
Pitfield, Milton Keynes, MK11 3LW, UK
UKHW021042200726
13857UKWH00003B/765

9 780557 274482